Energy EF1

Next Generation Tapping & Emotional Freedom Techniques

First Edition, 2012

Silvia Hartmann

DragonRising Publishing

United Kingdom

www.DragonRising.com

Energy EFT (Book & DVD): Next Generation Tapping & Emotional Freedom Techniques

© Silvia Hartmann 2012
1st Edition, 2012 (DVD Edition)
ISBN: 978-1-908269-25-6

Published By DragonRising Publishing
United Kingdom
www.DragonRising.com

Dedicated to

Gary Craig

The original creator of EFT Emotional Freedom Techniques.

Thank you for your gift.

Table of Contents

Part I - Learning EFT

Welcome To EFT Energy

EFT Emotional Freedom Techniques is a wonderfully simple and likewise, immensely profound method to remove blockages to success, health and happiness in our lives and to quite literally, re-energize us so we have the energy, the power, the inspiration we need.

Over the last 15 years, millions of people from all around the world, from all walks of life, old and young alike have found EFT to be a reliable, easy way to help themselves and others with problems of all kinds in a whole new way.

This new way really is a *new way*.

EFT may be using energy points and places that have been talked and written about for at least ten thousand years, but the way in which we apply modern EFT is something that has never been done in the history of humanity before.

In this way, EFT opens the doors to experiences we have never had before and this is tremendously exciting.

When we apply EFT to our problems, not only do the problems go away, but there is more.

We learn that we can become energized; that where there was fear, now there is courage and pride; where there was sadness and grief, now there is the freedom; and where there was anger and hatred, there can be love.

There is still more to it - when our emotions change, so do our thoughts and our bodies, as well.

When we feel energized, powerful and happy, our thinking becomes clearer, more logical; we gain access to the powers of our mind.

Likewise, when we are energized, our bodies become happier; they feel stronger, healthier, lighter and younger, too.

After all these years and all these experiences, it is still most wonderful to consider that so many good things can come from something as simple as EFT. All we have to do is to remove energy blockages from our energy body, and then go on to improve the flow of energy even further, and we really do become more energized in every sense of the word.

What is also wonderful about EFT and what sets it apart from the ancient forms of emotional control through energy work is that EFT is so personal for each one of us.

Instead of having to think and meditate on "off the peg" ideas or stand in a row to think the same thoughts and do the same movements as everyone else, we get to work with our own individual problems and challenges instead.

We get to choose what we want to treat, what we want to deal with; we get to have our say what we want out of life at last.

Each one of us is highly individual.

We were born all different to start with, and then our life experiences went on to shape us, make us more and more different with each day that passed, with each experience - good and bad alike - that was had.

So it stands to reason that each one of us has our own challenges, and our own order and sequence in which to approach these challenges as we go through life.

For some, EFT can help with health; for others, relationships are the most important issue. Someone else might want to address memories that haunt them first of all, and others may have life long problems with stress, addictions, low self esteem, sadness, grief or anger.

- **EFT allows us to direct its effects wherever we want to start, and whatever we want to apply it to.**

This is truly revolutionary and it is also what makes EFT so immensely effective.

Further, we don't have to wait around for the next "sacred circle time" of therapy or healing with EFT.

We can use EFT at any time, anywhere we go; and therefore, we can treat the daily upsets and the "stuff" that happens on an ongoing basis, again highly personalised, as and when we need it.

EFT is quite literally in your own hands.

Once you have learned the simple protocol, you own it; it is yours and it is yours to use, any time, anywhere. There are no expensive machines involved; there are no repeat prescriptions. EFT is yours to use forever, and freely share with others too, and all it takes is ten minutes to show someone what to do and where the treatment points are.

What a wonderful gift - we can hardly begin to appreciate this completely.

If you are new to EFT, we can also tell you that it gets better and better with practice and experience.

Even though EFT can help you feel better right away, especially if you don't stop too soon and keep tapping until you feel really energized (this is a core part of EFT Energy!), this is still only the beginning.

When we apply EFT, we quite practically step into a whole new world of possibilities and potential, far beyond the mere symptom cessation we currently crave.

In this book you will find the new EFT Heart & Soul Protocol, all the instructions and exercises you need to get started with EFT, as well as many examples how to apply EFT for different problems and challenges directly, simply and with excellent effect.

The most important piece of advice at the beginning is:

- **Simply start tapping!**

EFT works with real people who live in the real world, today, in the 21st Century. These are very different people to those who lived 6,000 years ago; we have challenges and experiences those who devised the ancient ways of working with energy could not have foreseen in their wildest dreams. We eat differently, act differently, think very differently and the range of problems we face on a daily basis were completely unknown back in the day when people lived in little villages, worked on farms and had their life's paths mapped out from the cradle to the grave, reliably.

Even if you had no luck with some of the older methods around, take heart and give EFT a fresh start.

Allow yourself to become fascinated by the EFT protocol, how it feels and how it affects you.

Pay attention even to small sensations, shifts and movements in your thoughts, body sensations and emotions - you are learning not just EFT, but important new things about yourself, how you work, how mind/body/spirit interact and influence each other in your own particular and absolutely unique case.

There are many wonderful aspects to the practice of EFT; that we start understand ourselves better and as a result, gain a better relationship with ourselves in the process is high on the list of benefits.

In this spirit, be gentle with yourself; follow the simple instructions, pay attention to your own stress levels and start by treating stress first of all so you are in a calm and curious state of mind when you start your own exploration of EFT and now, let us no longer delay and find out more about EFT, how it works, and how you can make it work for you.

How EFT Works

All human beings have an *energy body*.

What exactly one particular person's energy body is like, we do not know as we can't see or measure the energy body.

There are some basic things we can know about the energy body:

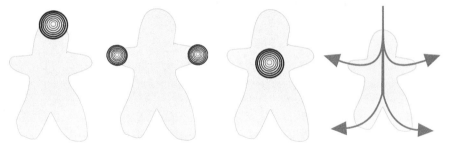

- This energy body has a head of energy, the *energy mind*;
- it has hands made from energy, the *healing hands*,
- it has energy organs such as the *heart centre*
- and it has many energy flows and *energy channels* that transport energy in, through and out the energy body.

ENERGY MUST FLOW

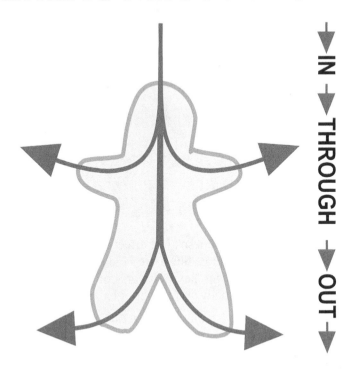

- In order to function properly, *energy must flow* freely **into** the energy body, **through** and **out**.

Sometimes, the flow of energy becomes blocked.

When this happens, problems arise in the energy body:

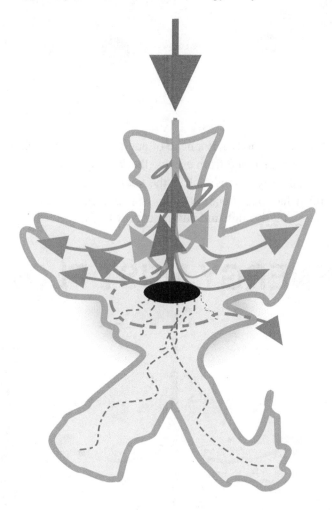

Please note how the blockage doesn't just affect the direct erea[1] of where it is located, but how all the energy flows are being disturbed and disrupted because of it. Energy blockages have all sorts of side effects and really throw the mind/body/energy body system out of balance.

If this energy blockage was removed, it is easy to understand how this person would feel much better - from relief at the top to having more energy at the bottom, and feel more "right" in themselves, and definitely more alive, more "energized."

1 erea - Short for "existing energetic reality."

In EFT,
we tap on certain energy points
to improve the flow of energy
and clear the blockages.

When the blockages are cleared, a person starts to feel different, better and more energized.

Emotions change, thoughts change, and many other things change as a result.

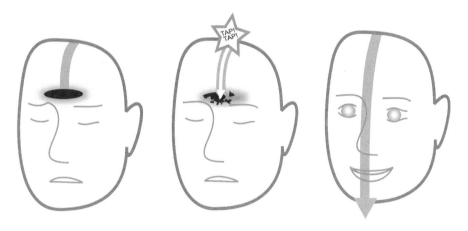

EFT Works By
Increasing The Flow Of Energy
Through The Energy Body.

When there is positive, powerful flow of energy through the energy body, we experience **positive emotions** - happiness, personal power, feeling good, feeling compassionate, feeling loving.

When the flow of energy in the energy system is disrupted, we feel **negative emotions** instead - stress, panic, anger, sadness and all the many different ways the real feelings in the physical body that are our emotions have been labelled.

- **When we tap on the energy points to improve energy flow in the energy body, we can unlock energy blockages.**

Energy flow improves, and we start to feel better.

We tap some more to improve the energy flow even further - and we get to feel even better still!

It is that simple, and because it is simple and true, EFT works so well and has helped so many people overcome so many problems.

Thereby, instead of trying to undo the thoughts or memories in some way, which has been attempted by millions in therapy for many years and with highly unpredictable results, by working with EFT at the real source of the problem, with the energy body, we finally have a real tool to "make us feel better" - for the first time in recorded human history.

As you will see, this simple yet profound discovery doesn't only make perfect sense, it has also proven itself in practice - there are now tens of thousands of therapists all across the world, daily relieving clients of all kinds of long standing problems using variations on this idea, successfully, predictably, time and time again. And just as importantly, there are many, many more individual people who are using EFT to help themselves feel better all around the world today.

Theory and conscious understanding is all good and well, but you don't really begin to appreciate the truth of how amazing and wonderful EFT is - until you have experienced it for yourself.

In a moment, we're going to learn how to do basic EFT, and you can pick any stress, limitation, fear or feeling that bothers you and try it out for yourself.

What Can We Treat With EFT?

EFT is not a "miracle cure."

EFT works by unblocking the flow of energy through the energy body. This gives us a different perspective and a different way to address old problems, and this is very important.

EFT can be expected to make significant changes in all problems that have their root in the energy body.

This includes first of all, all forms of emotions.

Emotions are the feedback devices
that tell us about
the conditions in the energy body.

- **Negative emotions correspond to disturbances and blockages in the energy body, causing us to feel "bad."**

- **Positive emotions correspond to the energy body flowing freely and feeling "great."**

Real emotions have a physical component. This means you can physically feel sensations of trembling, pressure, heat, churning, pounding, fluttering and so on in your physical body. These are messages from the energy body, transmitted through the physical body so we can do something about them, just the same as stepping on a rusty nail would hurt in the physical foot.

As so little was known about energy and emotions, people in the past didn't understand the connection between emotions and movements in the energy body. With EFT, we can reliably and predictably improve energy flow and that will cause us to "feel better" in the literal sense of the word.

- **Treating emotional disturbances, emotional stress and emotional pain is the first and most important application of EFT.**

Many if not all human problems have some form of emotional disturbance attached to them.

For example, when someone gets physically sick, they can also become scared and unhappy.

When we work with EFT to improve their emotions about being sick, and we improve the flow of energy through their energy body, we might not be healing their sickness, but we will make them feel better.

We will also release a lot of emotional stress from the whole person, so the body stands a better chance of repairing itself more quickly.

- **EFT does not treat physical illness.**

EFT can only treat the energy system components of a problem; but in doing so, many positive effects can happen.

- **Likewise, EFT does not treat physical pain.**

However, physical pain often has an energy or emotional component to it; when we release this with EFT, the experience of pain changes. This can lead to pain reduction, or the pain being experienced differently; we can't say in advance how the application of EFT will affect any one person.

We can certainly say that it is worth **trying EFT on *everything***.

The energy body aspects of any problem we have has never been addressed at all, and here is a whole third of the mind/body/spirit triad which is awaiting exploration.

EFT can bring forward movement into many, many stuck problems and can surprisingly solve many more.

We can also learn a lot by applying EFT to our problems. At the very least, with the emotional disturbances out of the way, we can get to a much more rational assessment of what else needs to be done to completely overcome a problem.

EFT is thereby not a miracle cure that can heal all ills of mankind, but it is a new approach that can bring surprising results and forward movement into all sorts of old, stuck problems.

EFT is quick, it's painless; improving the flow of energy through the energy body is always a good thing to do so we say:

"Try EFT On Everything!"

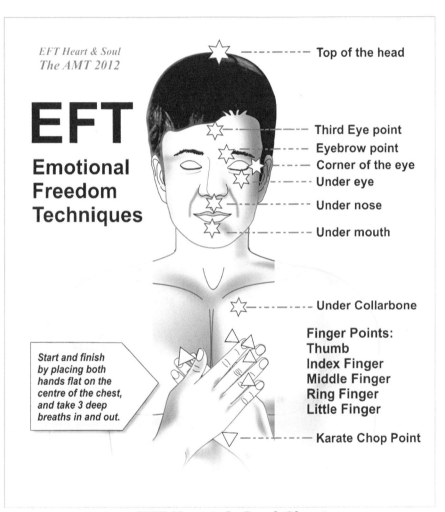

EFT Heart & Soul
The AMT 2012

EFT

Emotional Freedom Techniques

- Top of the head
- Third Eye point
- Eyebrow point
- Corner of the eye
- Under eye
- Under nose
- Under mouth
- Under Collarbone

Finger Points:
Thumb
Index Finger
Middle Finger
Ring Finger
Little Finger

- Karate Chop Point

Start and finish by placing both hands flat on the centre of the chest, and take 3 deep breaths in and out.

EFT Heart & Soul Chart

The EFT Round

EFT uses major energy centres and special energy points or meridian points to stimulate and improve the flow of energy through the energy body.

0 = **The Heart Centre**. This is where we start and finish our round of EFT by placing both hands flat on the centre of the chest in the Heart Healing Position and take three deep breaths in and out.

1. **Top Of The Head** - The highest point on the top of your head.
2. **Third Eye Point** - In the centre of your forehead.
3. **Start Of The Eyebrow** - Where the bone behind your eyebrow turns into the bridge of your nose.
4. **Corner Of The Eye** - On the bone in the corner of your eye.
5. **Under The Eye** - On the bone just below your eye, in line with your pupil if you look straight ahead.
6. **Under The Nose** - Between you nose and your upper lip
7. **Under The Mouth** - In the indentation between your chin and your lower lip
8. **Under The Collarbone** - In the angle formed by your collarbone and the breastbone
9. **Thumb** - all finger points are on the side of the finger, in line with the nail bed.
10. **Index Finger**
11. **Middle Finger**
12. **Ring Finger**
13. **Little Finger**
14. **Karate Chop Point** - on the side of your hand, roughly in line with your life line.

0 = And to finish the round of EFT, back to the **Heart Healing Position** where we take three deep breaths in and out.

Take a moment now go through the sequence, starting with the Heart Healing position where you take three deep breaths in and out. Then find and touch each point in turn with your index finger.

Touch each point lightly, breathe deeply and simply pay attention to how that feels, and how each point creates all kinds of different sensations you can feel in your body.

Tapping EFT

The EFT treatment points are stimulated by tapping lightly on them.

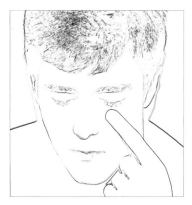

Even though we are using our physical hands on our physical body, we are not trying to massage muscles, bones or tissue but instead **it is our energy hands tapping on our energy body** which produce the results.

- **Each individual tap is like closing an electric circuit.**

As such, tapping "harder" doesn't do the trick; but tapping with awareness and paying attention to the contact between your fingertip and your body as you tap really helps.

You can tap with either hand on either side of the bilateral points. Normally people will tap with the index finger of their leading hand on the opposite side of the face. You can choose either side on the bilateral points.

Try now tapping the point under your eye, with your index finger, quite gently and rhythmically, as many times as it takes for you to take a normal breath in and out.

The strength of tapping should be light, just enough so that you feel a resonance from the tapping spreading out across a reasonable part of that side of your face when you pay close attention.

Different people have different speeds of tapping, and the speed of tapping often relates naturally to what we are tapping on. We generally show a tapping speed in the rhythm of "Jingle Bells."

For practice, turn back to the diagram on page 21.

Start with the Heart Healing position and tap all the points from the Top Of The Head to the Karate Chop point, ending up with the Heart Healing position at the end, right now to get the feel of doing EFT.

Remember to breathe deeply throughout and move towards finding a rhythm between the tapping and your breath so that the EFT round flows easily and smoothly all the way from the beginning to the end.

A single EFT round is from Heart Healing to Heart Healing, with all the points from the Top of the Head to the Karate Chop point in between.

Contacting The Problem

The most important part of any EFT treatment is to tune in on a problem correctly so that we know what we are tapping on.

To direct the unblocking effects to the required erea, we focus on the problem.

This can be done in various different ways, some of which we will discuss later. The simplest way of starting with EFT is by using a statement of the problem, for example: *"I am afraid of spiders."*

Preferably, this is spoken out loud to engage as much of the neurology as possible and to contact the problem as directly as possible.

- It is important to note at this point that the statement is not to be confused with an affirmation (*see also EFT & Affirmations in the A-Z of EFT*).

The energy system is a very complex environment. Each problem has its own unique address in that energy system - there is a blockage that corresponds to the problem.

We need to get to *this one specific blockage* rather than all the other many places, and we do this by consciously thinking towards the problem or "tuning in" on the problem.

- When we think about or tune in on a real problem, we can immediately notice that our feelings - the real sensations in our bodies - start to change.

This is the sign that there really is a problem, and it is affecting us physically as the energy body transmits how it feels through the medium of our emotions, the 6th sense of feeling energy movements that have no physical origin.

- We now give the problem a description to keep our attention on the problem while we tap, and this is our **set up** statement, for example, "I am afraid of spiders."

Now we assume the Heart Healing position, take three deep breaths in and out, and say out aloud, "I am afraid of spiders."

We then start tapping from the top of the head down, and on each point we tap, we can say the **set up** again, "I am afraid of spiders," or we can use a shortened **reminder phrase**, "Spiders" to keep us focused on the problem as we tap the whole round of EFT.

- The more simple, forthright, direct and truthful we can be in stating the problem, the more effective the EFT treatment becomes.

Here are a couple of stories to illustrate this point.

After a demonstration of EFT for a Weight Watchers group, a lady tried EFT with the set up of, "I'm not as thin as I would like to be," and said that she felt nothing when she tapped. When she was asked to consider if that was really what she thought when she looked in the mirror, and she shook her head and whispered, "No, I think I'm a fat cow."

When she tapped using that set up instead, the shift was extreme and the release visible to all and joyful in its intensity. She has since reported that this moment constituted a true turning point in her life and she has never thought about herself in such negative terms ever again since that day.

Another lady who was pregnant and afraid of giving birth, used the statement, "I am apprehensive of the forthcoming event." Again, nothing happened.

When she was asked to find a better description that would ring more true to her, she came up with, "The truth is that I'm scared to death of giving birth."

Tapping on this provided her with the release she so desperately needed, cured her backache and headache on the spot, and allowed her to continue forward with her pregnancy without further problems.

In a moment, take a little time to think about a problem that you have, a pain, a fear, an illness or perhaps a phobia, something that always makes you depressed when you think about it, just generally any negative emotion you are happy to release now and forever.

- Choose a set up statement that rings true to you, choosing simple, direct words that make sense to you.

- **The more forthright, direct and truthful you can be, the more profound a change you will experience.**

Understanding Stress

We have discovered in the long term use of EFT that when people are stressed, they say and think and do and feel all sorts of things they wouldn't say, think, do or feel if they weren't so stressed.

For example, a stressed person might say, "I can't cope, I don't have what it takes, I'll never succeed at anything, I'm just a loser, nobody loves me, nobody cares, nothing in my life ever goes right, God hates me and I wish I'd never been born!"

What we have here is a flood of "stress talk" - none of it is really true, none of it has any relevance or information about the real problems of this person, and none of this stress talk makes a good EFT set up statement.

- **Everybody starts to think crazy thoughts when they are too stressed.**

Under stress, everyone will generate what seem to be endless negative statements, and in the past people tapped and tapped using set ups from such stress talk and found little relief.

We have learned that in order to get a good EFT set up statement which clearly and precisely describes the problem so we can solve it, **we need to de-stress first.**

As soon as we start to de-stress, we can think more clearly.

In the example of our stressed person above, he was encouraged to just use "Stress!" as his set up statement. After the very first round of EFT, he had calmed down enough to say, "There is lot of pressure at work and it's driving me crazy ..." which is already much more promising than "God hates me!"

The next set up was "Pressure at work," which de-stressed this gentleman enough to be able to identify that it was one particular manager who was setting impossible deadlines and who was the "real problem."

 Using EFT to take off the top levels of stress first and before you formulate a set up for "the real problem" avoids doing many rounds on meaningless stress talk and gets you better results, every time.

Stress and Energy Flow

Stress is always a sign of blocked energy flow - the energy body becomes de-stabilised and that shows up in crazy thinking, irrational emotions and also in "body stupidity" such as clumsiness, shaking, becoming uncoordinated.

When we tap EFT, we remove blockages from the energy system and improve the flow of energy, and that lowers stress immediately.

99.9% of all people and even children in the modern world are much more stressed than we realise, and they are stressed all the time.

When stress becomes too high, we quite literally go crazy and can't help but make very bad decisions, think "fool thoughts" (such as, "Nobody loves me!") and experience all sorts of very disturbing emotions, from anger tantrums via panic attacks to crying fits.

In the past, people didn't realise just how much stress is to blame for all kinds of malfunctions in mind, body and spirit.

Many people still walk around today thinking they have "low self esteem" when in fact, they're just stressed quite literally out of their minds.

- **Using EFT to alleviate <u>general stress</u> is one of the healthiest and best things you can do for yourself, and teach others too, including friends, family and even young children.**

Very importantly, when we remove the disturbance of stress, we get to find out what our real problems are and we can get to work on them with EFT quickly and precisely. A student on the EFT Master Practitioner course likened this to melting away the snow so you can now discover the real rocks that were hiding underneath.

 We strongly recommend that any time you use EFT, start with a round or two to simply reduce stress, which will put you in a much better position to come up with good set ups to treat what is really a problem in your life.

The Set Up

Now that we have de-stressed enough to be able to name the real problem, we can start with the **Set Up** which consists of

- assuming the Heart Healing position,

- taking three deep breaths, in and out,

- and making the first set up statement out aloud

... which directs the treatment to the right place in your energy body.

 It is perfectly OK to start feeling feelings in your body as you make the set up statement, to feel angry or sad or low all of a sudden as you "tune in" to the problem.

These are the exact emotions we are going to be *releasing* by applying EFT to them, and these emotions are going to *change for the better* as we do our rounds of EFT.

Remember to:

- Breathe deeply, in and out, at least once on each point you tap; and

- Pay attention to the feelings in your body which tell you what's going on with your energy system.

If you are tuning in on a very disturbing problem with a high emotional charge, please de-stress more first if you are afraid or you are becoming overwhelmed.

 For very extreme emotional problems, we highly recommend you find a good EFT practitioner to be by your side.

No-one expects even the greatest dentist in the world to extract their own molars all by themselves; it is just common sense to seek assistance with extreme problems that cause so much stress that you can't be expected to deal with it all alone.

Seek assistance for extreme problems - it's the right thing to do.

The Complete EFT Round

Following the Set Up, we now tap all the points, starting from the Top of the Head and ending up with the Karate Chop Point on the hand, followed by assuming the Heart Healing position again for three deep breaths, in and out.

As you tap each point, repeat a shortened version of the Set Up Statement which is called the **reminder phrase**; so if your set up statement was,

"I'm so worried about my daughter Sandy."

… you can shorten this down to:

"So worried."

… on each point at the same time as you tap.

The reason for repeating the reminder phrase is that we can get distracted very easily; by repeating the reminder on each point we stop ourselves from thinking about lunch, the next appointment or how the weather has changed and make sure the tapping goes directly to the problem you're working on.

Once you know where the points are, the entire round of tapping should take no more than about 3 minutes, unless you feel a strong urge to stay longer on one particular point which can sometimes happen.

A note: As you start to tap, your feelings change and sometimes they change so much that you want to start changing the reminder phrase in the middle of a round. That is perfectly OK and a good sign that the problem is already changing, *evolving*.

Testing Your Changes

The SUE Scale - Subjective Units Of Experience *(Hartmann 2009)*

A great way to ascertain from yourself or others just how you feel is to put a number on it. The technical term is taking a SUE Level or SUE Scale reading, which stands for *Subjective Units of Experience*.

What that means is you ask yourself:

On a scale of -10 to +10,

- -10 being the highest imaginable pain/ upset/ distress/ fear/ sadness/ discomfort, and

- +10 being the highest level of joy/happiness/feeling great,

... where would you rate what you are experiencing at this moment?

Where are you on the SUE scale right now?

A tip: Sliding your finger over the scale and paying attention to what "feels right" can be a very helpful indicator.

You can use the SUE scale for measuring stress, the severity of emotions as well as for physical sensations and even for beliefs which might be a problem:

On the SUE Scale:

- how stressed are you right now?
- how depressed are you right now?
- how painful is your leg?
- how bad is your fear of heights?
- how distressing is this memory?
- how much do you love this person?
- how true or untrue is this statement?
- how happy are you right now?

Before you begin tapping for any subject or problem, take the time to take a SUE rating and make a mental note of it. Then, when you have completed a round of EFT, check the SUE scale again to find how much has changed.

This is also a good way to be able to assess how well the treatment has worked and if you need further rounds of EFT.

Sometimes, the problem can go from -10 to +10 in a single EFT treatment round. This is also known as the "EFT One Minute Wonder" or the "EFT Miracle" and it's awesome when that happens.

More often though, you start with a -7, and after a round of tapping, the severity is reduced to a -3 or -2.

- This means that the situation is evolving but there is more EFT to be done.

Also, and this is a unique feature of energy work, we don't stop at the "zero point of nothing" but we want to IMPROVE energy flow into the positive wing of the SUE scale. That's where we really start to feel better, come to life, and get close to "living life with a full battery," as one person described it.

Using the SUE scale helps keep your EFT treatments on track. It's a great way to measure your stress, measure your improvements, and to make sure you don't stop too early when just one more round could turn the EFT treatment from mere pain relief into a really exciting, energizing, healing experience.

- **A tip:** Use the SUE scale for one week to test your stress levels every day and tap to improve the flow of energy until you feel good and empowered, a high positive on the + side of the scale.

This will really help you develop a much better understanding of how stress and energy flow interact, and will make for a much better week.

Subsequent Treatment Rounds

If the original set up statement was, "I have this problem," you have tapped a first round on "this problem," and upon checking with yourself, this problem is not as severe any longer but still noticeable, change the set up to:

"I still have some of this problem."

When you're down to a rating of "Oh its a tiny little bit now!" which would be a -2, or -1 on the SUE rating scale, do the next round of EFT with the set up of,

"I want to completely overcome this problem now!"

When you get to the Zero Point of Nothing in the middle of the SUE scale, where the problem has gone and you don't feel anything about it any longer, it is time to think about how you want to feel. Now, instead of think about the problem, we want to think about what positive emotions or what kind of energy we want in our lives, and use these for our set ups instead, for example,

"I want to feel amazing!"

This takes you to the positive side of the SUE scale as you are starting to feel positive emotions as the energy flow improves.

Now to improve your energy flow even further and to bring up your SUE reading towards the high positive numbers (+7 and above) tap a round for,

"I want to feel EVEN MORE amazing!"

... or any positive phrase, want or desire that comes to your mind.

Really pay attention to how good it feels when energy flows better and enjoy the sensations!

And that's it! EFT is as simple as that.

There's no need for you to worry about getting it wrong, or getting the wrong set statement.

All EFT you do is good for you!

Any EFT you do stimulates the energy system, improves energy flow, releases old energy blockages, relaxes you, calms you and makes you feel better. With practice, you'll get much better at spotting good set ups and your EFT will go from strength to strength.

The Healing Event

You might have heard and read many EFT stories about people tapping for something, and then something amazing happened.

Not only did the problem disappear instantly, there was a moment of enlightenment where everything changed. Not only had the problem completely disappeared, the person was amazed and excited, quite literally jumping for joy. It is precisely these kinds of *Healing Events* that have inspired so many people to take up EFT and want to share this joy with other people.

Also known as the "One Minute Wonder" and the "EFT Miracle," these lightning strikes of healing are simply what we now call energy "Healing Events."

A major blockage is taken out of the energy system and all of a sudden, energy can flow freely again, often the first time in a long time, and there's a rush of energy which was trapped behind the blockage, causing that amazing "lightning strike" sensation which truly is an event[2]. Once you have felt that, the world will never be the same again; and we now think of these Healing Events as true "enlightenment experiences."

What was so mysterious before has become quite simple. It's just like finding the one light bulb in a chain of Christmas tree lights and giving it a little tap and in an instance, there is a bright flash as all the lights come on when there was only darkness before.

The Healing Event is the biggest difference between energy work and other forms of therapy.

- **Every time we tap EFT, we always seek a Healing Event.**

When we improve energy flow step by step using the SUE scale and bringing it up higher and higher, one tap at a time, one round of EFT at a time, **a Healing Event <u>has to happen</u> eventually.**

It structurally can't not happen - once energy flow reaches a certain level, that breakthrough has to occur and the Healing Event comes into being.

When that has happened, the problem as it was will never come back in its old form. It really is solved, once and for all. We can say as well that until the Healing Event has happened, the problem isn't solved completely, it can come back and then we have to tap on it again.

---

2   Events are high energy, lightning strike like experiences that change the energy system in a heartbeat, and forever.

We always seek the Healing Event, but that doesn't mean we have to be disappointed if it doesn't happen in the first couple of taps, or even in the first session.

- **As long as we keep improving the energy flow, we're heading in the right direction, towards the Healing Event.**

We sum this up by saying, "You don't have to solve it, only evolve it!"

A single point movement on the SUE scale towards the positive side and the +10 is a step in the right direction.

Keep improving the energy flow, and the Healing Event will have to come in the end. It's great if that happens in one tap, or one session; but it is just as good if it takes two or three sessions.

Keep improving the flow of energy, and you're heading in the right direction towards the Healing Event, that enlightenment moment of real change which is the hallmark and the gift of modern energy work.

"You don't have to solve it, only evolve it!"

Improve Your Energy Flow

For practice, now have a go at improving your energy flow with EFT.

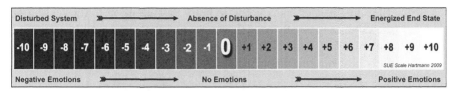

Disturbed System	»	Absence of Disturbance	»	Energized End State
-10 -9 -8 -7 -6 -5 -4 -3 -2 -1	**0**	+1 +2 +3 +4 +5 +6	+7 +8 +9 +10	

SUE Scale Hartmann 2009

Negative Emotions	»	No Emotions	»	Positive Emotions

Start by finding a number of how stressed you are overall, right now.

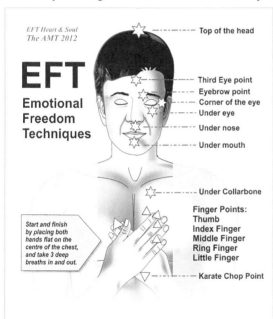

EFT Heart & Soul
The AMT 2012

EFT

Emotional Freedom Techniques

- Top of the head
- Third Eye point
- Eyebrow point
- Corner of the eye
- Under eye
- Under nose
- Under mouth
- Under Collarbone

Finger Points:
Thumb
Index Finger
Middle Finger
Ring Finger
Little Finger

Start and finish by placing both hands flat on the centre of the chest, and take 3 deep breaths in and out.

Karate Chop Point

Now do a full round of EFT, starting and finishing with the Heart Healing position, with the Set Up of "Release stress!" and the reminder phrase, "Stress" as you tap on each point.

Breathe deeply in and out as you tap slowly and mindfully.

When you have completed the round of EFT, check your level on the SUE scale - what is your number now?

When you have reached 0, do the next round for, "I want to improve my energy flow!" as the Set Up in the Heart Healing position, with the reminder phrase of, "Energy!"

Repeat until you get into the positive side of the SUE scale.

Pay attention how this makes you feel, the real feelings in your body.

- Practice this simple **stress → calm → feeling positive** basic EFT treatment. It will teach you how to do EFT.

- Once you have learned how it works, you can then apply EFT to your specific problems.

Tips On Tapping

- It is your energy hands tapping on your energy body which is doing the work in EFT. To know this helps to activate your "healing hands" and improves results.

- Tapping "harder" isn't going to help. Pay attention to the feeling of the contact between your fingertips and your body; tapping should feel pleasant and relaxing to you. Experiment with how tapping feels best for you personally.

- Tap lightly and rhythmically, using your index finger.

- Breathe deeply in and out while you tap. Always take time for one deep breath in and out between points.

- Keep relaxed as you tap. Loosen your shoulders, relax your face, your neck and your arms, your wrist, hand and fingers as this helps with energy flow.

- Move your body a little to keep it loose and relaxed as you tap.

Alternatives To Tapping

Instead of tapping, you can also stimulate the points by massaging them gently, and simply by touching them.

- Try for yourself a round of EFT with gently massaging the points instead of tapping;

- and a round of EFT where you place your index finger on the points and breathe in deeply on each point.

Massaging and holding the points can be a good alternative if you have a headache, for example, a toothache, or you would like to reflect deeply on a topic.

If in doubt, just tap.

General Tips On Improving Energy Flow

There are three things which can help improve energy flow when you are doing an EFT session.

The first is breathing.

When we become stressed, we start breathing irregularly and shallow; reminding yourself to breathe deeply really improves energy flow.

Sometimes it can be very beneficial to step outside for a moment of breathing fresh air, or opening a window to let some fresh air in.

The second is movement.

Move your body, relax your shoulders and neck.

Sometimes it really helps to get up and shake out your hands and feet to encourage energy flow; but in general, pay attention to any parts of your body that feel locked up, tense or tight. Taking a moment to make movements to "unlock" tight muscles and sinews can really help your EFT sessions along.

The third tip is to have some water handy and drink a few sips in between treatment rounds.

This also helps to wake up your body and your energy system and adds extra fresh energy as well as avoiding getting dehydrated if you are doing a number of EFT treatment rounds on a particular problem.

EFT - The Whole Treatment At A Glance

Before you start: Are you very stressed? If so, do a round or two simply on "Stress!" to relieve stress from your energy system and so you can think more clearly. When you are ready:

Step 1 - Name the problem, clearly, directly and truthfully.

Step 2 - Take a SUE reading of how bad it is right now.

Step 3 - Assume the Heart Healing Position, take three deep breaths in and out and say the set up statement out aloud..

Step 4 - Repeat the set up statement or a shortened reminder phrase and say this on each point as you tap from the Top of the Head to the Karate Chop point. Always take one deep breath, in and out, before moving on to the next point.

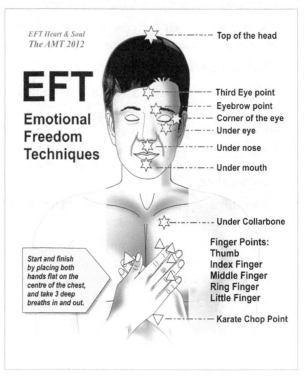

EFT Heart & Soul
The AMT 2012

EFT

Emotional Freedom Techniques

Top of the head

Third Eye point
Eyebrow point
Corner of the eye
Under eye
Under nose
Under mouth

Under Collarbone

Finger Points:
Thumb
Index Finger
Middle Finger
Ring Finger
Little Finger

Karate Chop Point

Start and finish by placing both hands flat on the centre of the chest, and take 3 deep breaths in and out.

Step 5 - Return to the Heart Healing position and take three deep breaths, in and out..

Step 6 - Take a new SUE reading. Any movement up towards +10 is good!

Subsequent Rounds - Choose a new set up to remove any remaining energy blockages so the problem goes down to zero. Then - Do more rounds of EFT to improve the energy flow beyond zero and into the positive wing of the SUE scale, all the way up to +7 or above.

Congratulations!
You have learned how to do EFT!

Part 2 - EFT Self Help

Setting Up For EFT Success

One of the truly marvellous things about EFT is that everyone who teaches or writes about or who practices EFT with clients also treat themselves with EFT in self help.

EFT is an extraordinary tool for human beings above all else, and the challenges of self treatment are much the same, regardless of whether you are an EFT guru or you've picked up this book for the very first time.

In the following chapters, we will be finding out how we can make our EFT self help treatments as easy, powerful and effective as possible.

There are certain things an EFT practitioner provides for their clients which we have to address in self help treatments as well, so let's start by taking a look at these important support structures so we can use them for excellent EFT self help.

- **Hold a positive attitude to the client.**

In self help, of course, you are the client. And all clients need to be treated with respect, with compassion, with love, with support, with a very positive attitude, in other words.

We need to make sure that the client is as stress free as possible, and that we treat them gently and lovingly throughout.

So by all means watch yourself and remind yourself to be nice. De-stress more if you find yourself getting frustrated or disappointed with your progress. Spend a little more time in the Heart Healing position to centre. Tap yourself lovingly, like you would touch a person you really deeply care for and want to support to the best of your abilities.

That's always good advice for any kind of treatment of the self, but with EFT energy work it particularly pays off in smoother and faster, more successful treatments.

- **Encourage the client.**

Encouragement and positive feedback is an essential part of helping a client relax and have a great EFT experience. In self help we bring in this energy by talking to ourselves out aloud throughout the treatment rounds.

Always speak the set up statement out aloud and the reminder phrases too, it helps you focus and engages your neurology much more.

Not speaking the phrases out aloud and losing focus as the mind races from one thing to another is one of the main reasons why self treatments can fail.

Remind yourself to breathe, move, and drink water in between treatment rounds. Once again, speak out aloud, "My breathing has gone shallow, I need to take a few deep breaths here ..." That is very helpful to keep you on track and doing the right things.

Allow yourself to be demonstrative. Make gestures, noises, exclamations, speak your mind and let your body speak as if a practitioner was with you and you want to share with them what's going on inside.

Remember this is about staying on track and improving energy flow through your body. The more you can support yourself on the EFT journey from problem to feeling much, much better, the easier that journey will be.

- **Keep the client on track.**

Other than general stress treatments and "in the moment" treatments, EFT works best when you decide what you want to work on and then see it through from the beginning to the end. This is what would happen if you told an EFT practitioner about your problem, and they would help keep you on track to solve that problem we came with at the start all the way through to the Healing Event.

When we work by ourselves, it can happen that we simply hop from one thought, memory and feeling to the next in a very haphazard fashion. In the past, people have tapped hundreds of rounds on this, that and the other, shaving a little bit off the discomfort here and there but never properly finishing any of it, never properly resolving any of it, and most importantly, never experiencing the true power of the Healing Event at the end.

When an EFT practitioner is there to help, first they will help us clarify what we want to working on, which is the first step towards solving that particular problem.

They can keep us on track; in the absence of that, we recommend to write down the problem on a piece of paper so you have it in front of you, for example, "I am afraid of spiders."

Staying on track with one particular problem and to see it through to its solution - the Healing Event! - is really important to gain the wonderful benefits from your EFT self treatments.

- **Make a note of other important topics that arise.**

When you start to tap, and energy starts to flow, so do thoughts, feelings, ideas and memories as well. You might for example remember a childhood incident about not getting a birthday present. Rather than switching horses in mid-stream and now starting to tap for this instead of the problem you started out with, you can write that down on another piece of paper for a future treatment session and come back to the problem we're dealing with, namely the fear of spiders.

You can collect ideas for future treatments on these pieces of paper and put them into your EFT treatment bowl (or box, vase, etc.) for later. This is a good way of dealing with troublesome things when you don't have the time to work on them there and then. Later, when you do have time, you can pick out a problem at random and tap on it. If you get disrupted before a real Healing Event has happened, simply place the piece of paper with the problem back in the bowl so you can pick it up again and finish it completely.

Also, you will often find that some treatments also solve other problems. By looking through your EFT bowl every so often you can notice directly when "a problem has ceased to be a problem" and take out the piece of paper.

People who have made a collection of potential things to tap on in their EFT bowl have also commented how looking at the different problems all together and putting them physically into perspective can be helpful to uncover connections between all sorts of symptoms, problems and root causes.

Reviewing what's in the EFT bowl every so often and updating set ups and problems is in and of itself extremely interesting and can help you keep your personal development on track in a whole new way.

- **Don't let the client stop too soon!**

This is very important. Just shaving off a few points on the SUE scale might feel like that's all you need or want to do, but it's not.

You really need to get the energy flow going enough so you start to feel more than just relief or "peace" or the absence of negative feelings.

The fact that we can go from the negative minus numbers on the scale beyond the zero point of nothing and into the positive + numbers, where the good, healthy experiences are to be found, is the great gift of modern energy work.

Don't waste this precious opportunity for real healing and change, and don't ever be satisfied with second best.

Without a practitioner there to encourage you to take that extra step, to remind you that if you feel spacey or sleepy, you're not on the positive wing of the SUE scale yet and at least one more round of energizing EFT is now needed, you have to have the will and discipline to take your EFT treatments to the best conclusion possible - and that is good energy flow and good feelings on the high end of the SUE scale, +7 and above.

Keep your focus on that white, light filled end of the scale and really desire to go there - that's where health is, where happiness lies, that's the only right place to be.

Do one more round, just for "Energy!" if necessary to really get your energy system moving. This is what brings you back to life, wakes you up, gives you clarity and logic in your thinking, and powerful, em-powered feelings and sensations in your body.

- **Refer the client to a more experienced EFT practitioner if this is necessary.**

Really do think of yourself as your client, a person you are responsible for and you want to help them as much as possible and in the best way.

There are some topics and problems which have so much emotional disturbance around it, they are too difficult to handle for a beginner in self treatment, or even any person, even if they are EFT Master Trainers.

If your problems are such that you feel overwhelmed at the thought of doing an EFT session for them, and this overwhelm has not receded after some de-stressing rounds of EFT for "This problem overwhelms me!" there is no shame whatsoever in getting help.

Call an experienced EFT practitioner for a session. Two heads are better than one, and real modern energy work should never be scary or painful in any way.

We always de-stress and build a pain free path to the heart of the problem every time.

- **Remind the client that EFT home treatments are of the essence.**

EFT is not just about mega sessions where mega problems are being resolved. The real beauty of EFT is that we can treat ourselves in the context and in the flow of our daily lives, to release stress and energize ourselves at any time this is necessary.

An EFT practitioner will always encourage their client to use EFT home treatments, and discusses with their clients what kind of easy set ups would be most helpful in between full EFT sessions.

As such, in self help you need to discuss with yourself what home treatments would be the most helpful at this time. A simple set up that is easily remembered and globally applicable, such as, "Energy!" or "Love," or "Joy," or just "Stress Away!" which can be done often and immediately is the best kind for home treatments. Thinking about what kind of positive energy forms will be most useful to you at this time is also a great way to end your EFT self help sessions and make them much more effective overall.

The final important advice for EFT self help is:

- **Be kind to the client!**

Be nice to them. Be patient. If your patience wears thin, treat yourself with EFT so you can be more compassionate, more loving and more logical as you think about the next step in "your client's" treatments.

Stop and think once in a while, "If this person we're treating here was someone I really loved, deeply and profoundly, what would I advise them to tap on next? How would I treat them? How can I encourage them more?"

The additional dimensions of care and compassion that come in when we think about treating someone else rather than "ourselves" is where the key to real EFT self help success lies, so in all your tapping, do remember **you are the client who deserves the best in loving care**, and be kind above all else.

Creating Successful EFT Set Ups

The most important part of successful EFT treatments is to make a good set up for the treatment.

Generally, the simpler and more direct a set up is, the more likely it is to produce a good result when we tap on it.

It is important to remember that we are treating disturbances and blockages in the energy body.

These blockages and disturbances are directly responsible for our negative emotions but also for stumbling blocks of all kinds in performance, thinking, feeling and doing.

We can feel these blockages quite physically in our bodies in the form of trembling and shaking; sensations of pressure, heaviness; feelings of coldness and tightness; churning in the stomach, pressure in the head and so on and so forth.

It is really important to understand that **emotions are real feelings.**

Emotions are not just in the mind, they can be felt in the body and that's what identifies a real emotion - you can feel physical sensations but there is no physical origin.

For example, a person who was fired from their work unexpectedly described this as "if I had been punched in the stomach."

There was no physical fist to cause that sensation; only a person across a desk saying the words, "Pack up your stuff, you're fired."

This experience triggered a reaction in the energy body, in and around the area of the stomach, and this produced the sensation of pain in the stomach.

All emotions work in that way.

Strong emotions are physically painful and the strongest emotions are so painful that we can no longer distinguish them from actual physical pain. These emotions are called psychosomatic pain and denote a very serious problem in the energy system.

We have also all kinds of more subtle sensations and emotions.

When you begin with EFT, we suggest to try it on problems you can really feel in your body. This is because such problems which cause painful emotions really need to be treated as soon as possible; but also because it is really easy to notice how these strong sensations begin to change when we apply EFT.

In general, the golden rule for successful EFT set ups is that they should have an emotional charge behind them, that you can physically feel there is something there that needs to be treated.

Tapping on "nothing" produces nothing - obviously.

Tapping on something produces something of a change.

Tapping on something profound and important produces profound and important changes.

- **The emotional charge is important, not any particularly clever choice of words.**

Don't Tap On Stress Talk

As we have noted, when people become stressed, they will naturally generate a flood of "stress talk."

This is a whole lot of negative things "spewing out" in a pretty endless list that might get worse and worse as the stress gets higher and higher.

If you find yourself in such an emotional state that "everything is terrible" and it sounds like a long laundry list of complaints and misery, you are very stressed and you need to treat yourself for STRESS, first of all.

Use the de-stressing EFT rounds we discussed in the chapter on "Improving Your Energy Flow" first of all until you have calmed down enough to be able to identify what exactly you are so upset about.

For example, there was a young lady who was very upset about her boyfriend and she cried, "He's a heartless bastard! He doesn't love me! He doesn't care about me! Why do I always choose the wrong men? What's wrong with me? Why am I such an idiot? I wish I was dead!"

Even though every one of these might sound like a good set up for an EFT treatment, that's clearly just stress talk and nothing else. After this lady had treated herself for stress, two rounds in all, she was able to identify what had caused her emotional meltdown in the first place. She had send her boyfriend a lengthy and highly meaningful text message to which he had responded with, "No time now busy will call later x."

She had felt shocked, upset and rejected when she received this, and by using the set up of, "Shocked, upset and rejected!" for the next EFT treatment round, she managed to solve a problem that she then realised had been "pretty much the story of her life up until today!"

She improved energy flow into the positive side of things by tapping a couple of rounds on, "I'm a lovable person," and finally, "I love me - and so do other people including my boyfriend!" which saved the day, the relationship, and many other problems in the future, too.

- **When you are very stressed or very emotionally upset, do a few treatment rounds simply for "stress" first.**

It will save you a lot of time in the long run and really help you formulate better, more precise and more powerful set up statements, especially in self help.

Use Your Own Words

When we train EFT practitioners, we always tell them how important it is to use a person's own words - the way they normally speak, the words they use, and never anything artificial or complicated.

When you do EFT in self help treatments, the same rule applies - use the words you would normally use to describe the problem.

It really is quite simple, even though we do get people asking, "I have a headache - what set up should I use?"

The set up is clearly, "I have a headache!" to get started.

- **Don't over think your problems or your set ups.**

The more direct, forthright and honest you can be, the better the set up will work.

Be Specific

EFT works best when we apply it to a specific problem, a specific emotion, a specific feeling or a specific moment in time.

"I have a headache!" is a fair enough set up to get started; it will certainly help relieve stress and you might be able to feel it lifting slightly, shifting slightly.

A more specific set up can then be made, for example, "I feel a pressure on the left hand side of my head just above my left eye," with a shortened reminder phrase of, "Pressure above my eye."

That's a specific location and after a round of EFT treatment, you might find that the pressure has moved, changed to a different location and might not be quite as intense as it was.

Make the next set up specific again, "I feel a light pain on the left side of my head, just over my ear," with a set up of, "Light pain over the left ear."

These "moving sensations" are actually energy blockages sliding along a pathway, a meridian for example, and they need to leave the energy body altogether. When they're all the way out, the headache will have gone, too.

You finish the treatment with a nice specific positive treatment for what you would like to feel instead of the headache, for example, "I want my head to feel light and bright," with a reminder phrase of "Light and bright!" to get to the positive wing of the SUE scale.

- **Being specific works for all sorts of other types of problems just the same.**

For example, instead of using a global set up such as, "I'm a terrible mother!" think about a specific incident that illustrates that problem. In this example, it was the fact that the lady in question had forgotten to pick up her son in time from play school and the teachers had made her feel really bad with their looks and sighs. She made the set up of, "The teachers made me feel bad with their looks and sighs," and the reminder phrase of "Looks and sighs," made her feel much better. When she got onto the positive scale with, "I'm a very good mother and I love my son," she realised that she had been very stressed and that she needed to pay more attention to her stress levels so she could pick him up on time in future more reliably.

Working with EFT and energy flow, we don't just "tap our bad feelings away." That's not and never the whole story; using EFT is about being able to do things more reasonably, more logically, and have the energy to do things right.

The lady who was so stressed that she forgot to pick up her son from play school on time didn't just tap the feeling of being a bad mother away; she also realised why she had been late and what she needed to do to avoid that in future, to do better, as it were.

In this way, we can use the systemic structure of EFT not just to feel better, but to do better in future as well, and that's very important.

Going back to the importance of being very specific when we make set ups for EFT treatments, here is another example, and this works with all memories.

"I am afraid of flying," is a global statement that will take off some top level stress, but it isn't specific enough to really solve the problem once and for all. You need one specific memory to find a good set up statement, for example a recent experience of being afraid of flying. When exactly did that happen? Where exactly did that happen? How did it get started?

In this example, the person said, "The last time I got really scared was when I was on a flight to Amsterdam, I was nervous anyway and when we were taking off, the plane all of a sudden seemed to drop, like on a fairground ride, and I felt like I was shooting out of myself in sheer panic."

"I felt like I was shooting out of myself in sheer panic," makes a very good set up and the reminder phrase would be, "Shooting out of myself."

Here is an example of being very specific, this time the problem is hay fever that came on suddenly in a 53 year old gentleman who never had it before in his life.

What was happening in his life at that time? He had just been diagnosed with skin cancer. Was there a special moment that he remembers, a moment when everything changed? This gentleman said, "Oh I remember that well enough. I was in the doctor's office and he said there were two types of cancer, one that's harmless and the other is deadly, and you have the second type! I don't remember much after that, the next thing I remember I am standing in the car park in front of a rhododendron bush in full bloom and I'm shaking, and I can't breathe ..."

This is a good time to remind ourselves that EFT does not cure cancer, or even hay fever. EFT works with the energy system and helps to heal the energy body, takes out blockages and reversals to the healthy flow of energy through the energy body.

This has effects on the body through the medium of the emotions - those physical sensations that have no physical origin. We cannot "scientifically prove" the connection between the shock of being told you have a deadly cancer, and being unable to breathe in front of a rhododendron bush not much later and the sudden onset of hay fever, but on a human level, it makes perfect sense that these things are related to one another.

"I was crying in front of the flower bush," was the set up and the reminder phrase was just, "Crying."

As you can imagine, this gentleman started to cry as he was tapping through the round.

Please note that this is a normal and natural occurrence when blocked energies get freed up and pressure begins to be released. Indeed, crying is a natural pressure valve for the energy system; and this gentleman said after his first round of EFT that he had not cried since that day. He also tapped for the news he was given in such an unfortunate way and as you can imagine, this released a lot of stress he had been carrying for two years.

EFT may not be able to cure cancer or hay fever (although the hay fever did seem to miraculously disappear after the treatment and has not returned as far as we know) but by removing stress from the energy body, it stands to reason that the body has more of a fighting chance as the gentleman goes through the various stages of his treatments and that must be a good thing.

Our final example on being very specific relates to a limiting belief. Here, we have a teenager who believes that he can't learn maths. He has much evidence of this, including bad marks in every maths test he has ever taken, an inability to understand maths questions, and failure across the board in maths activities in school, with private tutors and others who have tried to help over the years.

"I can't learn maths," is a global statement that releases some top level stress but we need something more specific that this to really solve the problem. What happens exactly when he is faced with a maths book or a maths problem? The young man said, "It's like everything goes dark, my head hurts and then I start to freak out."

The first round was on, "Everything goes dark and my head hurts," with a reminder phrase of "Head hurts." The second round was even more specific, "My head hurts like there's hands pushing in on my skull on the temples." These are direct descriptions of a form of emotion that doesn't have the usual labels like anger, sadness, fear or pain; but they are the same thing. There is something wrong with the energy system in the area around his head and energy flow needs to be restored to that area - urgently.

Tapping on "The hands pushing in on my skull," with a reminder phrase of "Pushing in at the temples," started to shift the sensation, and a few rounds of EFT later, with the headache successfully removed, the young man could look at a maths book without pain for the first time in 12 years. He commented on how brightly coloured the cover was, could open it and even said he was quite interested in finding out how it all worked, now that he could see the figures and signs clearly and his head didn't hurt any longer.

The original belief of, "I can't do maths," had changed to, "I can learn anything I want to, I have a good brain!" which is a reflection of the changes at the energy levels.

To sum up: When you try to find a good set up, you can start with a global statement of the problem. It will help you de-stress and then you will be able to home in on the problem by using very specific examples of the problem in action.

- **The more specific you can be, the better EFT will work for you.**

Stay On Track!

The biggest challenge for in depth EFT self help sessions is to stay on track. That means to take one problem all the way from the problem to the Healing Event without getting side tracked along the way.

The first step is to make up your mind what it is you are going to be tapping on; which problem you want to work with on this occasion.

If you are unclear, start with general stress relief first and treat yourself to at least two rounds just for, "Stress!" following with one round for, "Energy!"

You can choose words that suit you better but the idea is to release stress and energize yourself before you start working on the problem of the day.

When you are feeling clear, energized and ready for action, think about the problem and give it a title. This is not a set up; it is the description of the problem we want to solve, for example, "Grief over my breakup with Peter," or "I want to get over my money reversals," or, "I really want to sort out my problems with confidence."

Write this out on a piece of paper in clear, legible letters and put the paper somewhere where you can see it easily.

Now you can start thinking about set ups and do your first EFT treatment rounds. At the end of each round, and regardless what you were tapping on, you can come back to your description of the problem and ask yourself, "Is this completely resolved yet? Is there something else I need to tap on?"

This way, no matter where you go in your memories, no matter which emotions you experience, you can come back to the real reason this session is happening, and you can be sure that the problem gets solved properly.

If you come across another topic or issue whilst you tap, something you know that needs to be dealt with but is not directly related to the problem at hand, you can write that down on a fresh piece of paper and put it aside for later treatments.

You can collect all such pieces of paper in an EFT treatment bowl; this is a very useful thing in its own right as we have already discussed.

Also, should something disrupt your time or you run out of time, you can keep the paper with the "not yet completely resolved problem" for another session.

- **It is really important to take each and every problem through to a real Healing Event, a +8 on the SUE scale or higher.**

In the past, people used to "tap down" their various problems from a -9 to a -3. At this point, they would lose the plot and start thinking of other problems which were worse (such as any other problem that is worse than a -3). They would then switch away from the original problem which didn't get solved properly, and do the same to the new problem, which *also* didn't get solved properly. This would happen over and over again, and in spite of hours of tapping, in the end, not very much has been accomplished.

 Until and unless there was a real Healing Event, the problems will come back, and then we have to tap on them yet again, and again. This is why it is so important to really stay on track and take each and every problem through to a Healing Event.

When you have reached the Healing Event on the problem, you can throw the piece of paper away. Some people like to burn them as a part of the celebration of having really "gotten over this" for good; others like to collect them in a "Problem Solved!" folder.

Either way, to think about the problem before you start, to give it a title, to write it down and to keep referring back to it is an excellent way to keep your EFT self help on track and make good progress with your problems.

Write it down, stay on track!

Try EFT On Everything!

One of the really amazing things about EFT is that you can use it for every imaginable problem a human can possibly have.

We can't guarantee that something dramatic will happen in every case; but the fact is that no matter how long you've been trying to solve problem x, y or z, it has never been addressed at the energy body levels before.

The energy body has not been a reality for Western civilisation raised human beings for hundreds, if not thousands of years. Nobody has really tried to understand it, to help it or to find out how we can have a fully functional energy body.

As a result, we don't know what effects energy body treatments have on the various problems we experience.

As we've noted, of course EFT is the right type of treatment for emotional problems of all kinds.

But what about other kinds of problems?

In the previous chapters, we encountered a lady who thought she was a bad mother, a gentleman who was afraid of flying; another who had been diagnosed with cancer and hay fever, a person with a headache and a teenager who believed he couldn't do maths.

That's a huge variety of presenting problems already, and we've only just started on our adventure with EFT!

There are so many other problems.

Take addictions, for example. Surely, a physical addiction to cocaine, heroin or nicotine is immune to an energy body treatment such as EFT?

Or what about a strictly physical illness such as arthritis, or physical pain after breaking a leg or having a major operation? What about character traits such as being easily excitable, introverted or lazy?

The fact is that we just don't know how small or large the influence on the energy body is on any presenting problem.

We would say after many years of experience with EFT and many surprises along the way that you really should try EFT on *everything*.

The worst that can happen is that you feel more relaxed, and instead of feeling miserable, you start to feel a little bit more energized.

Far more often, we end up very surprised just how much better we can feel, how we can improve our performance, and how much we can learn about ourselves in the process.

Whatever your problem/s may be, just have a go.

Remember the basic guidelines of

- De-stressing first so you think more clearly;

- Be specific

- Use direct, honest, simple statements

... to make your set ups and allow yourself to be surprised.

You Don't Have To Solve It, Only Evolve It!

This headline is a very important part of working with EFT and energy.

Most of our energy problems exist because there's something stuck in the energy system; something is blocking the free flow of energy in, through and out our energy bodies.

When we start out with our EFT treatments, we all hope that we will experience a "one minute wonder," as in the much told story of Mary and her water phobia.

This lady had a severe phobia of water and would have anxiety attacks at the thought of getting wet; even an inch of water at the bottom of a bath tub would absolutely terrify her.

During a session with energy tapping pioneer Dr Roger Callahan who had been trying to treat her unsuccessfully with standard psychology methods for a long time, he asked her to tap as she talked about her fear. All of a sudden she leapt up from the treatment chair, cried, "It's gone!" and ran out into the garden to the swimming pool.

A lifelong problem - one tap under the eye, and it goes POOF!

This is absolutely true, and this really sometimes happens. When it does, that's wonderful.

But don't despair when instead of an instant enlightenment experience, you "only" get an improvement from -7 to -5 on the SUE scale.

- We call that an **evolution**; the problem is not stuck where it was any longer, it has changed, it has *evolved*.

This proves to us immediately that this problem can be moved by energy work and all we have to do is basically to keep on tapping, and it will eventually be resolved altogether.

Just keep moving the problem towards the 0 on the SUE scale, then keep moving it further into the positive side where our energy system starts to work as it is meant to work, as it was designed to work in the first place.

- **Keep evolving the problem, and it will resolve.**

That's what we mean by "You don't have to solve it, only evolve it!"

Get some forward movement on your stuck problem, and you're on the right track. You're doing the right thing and all you have to do is to keep on tapping. Don't give up too easily. In fact, don't give up!

Keep tapping.

Try some different set ups and if you're really stuck, try a round or two of EFT on "I'm really stuck!" to get some traction and some forward movement.

If the worst comes to the worst, call an experienced EFT practitioner and get not just their expertise but importantly also their energy involved in solving the problem.

Even small forward movement is 100 times better than staying stuck, so it's well worth doing. Also remember that a single round of EFT takes no more than three minutes; so it isn't that essential that you should get the best possible set ups today, or even tomorrow.

 As you practice with EFT and your experience with good set ups and reminder phrases naturally grows, you'll find it easier and easier to formulate good set ups.

The golden rule is, if you're confused and unsure on what your set ups should be, relax.

De-stress. Re-energize yourself.

There is no need to panic, you have time to try out different set ups and learn from them how to do it well, and you don't have to solve all your problems overnight -

"You don't have to solve it, only evolve it."

The EFT Experience

Unless you are familiar and experienced with modern energy work, doing EFT is quite unlike anything else you may have done before.

It isn't psychology; it isn't meditation, and it isn't hypnosis.

EFT produces noticeable changes in our emotions, which means in the feelings in our body.

These feelings are not "all in the mind," they are absolutely physical and "use the body" to make themselves known.

As a result, EFT produces a variety of body states and body occurrences.

Something which is very common is rumbling in the stomach and burping as energy flow improves and tensed muscles start to relax or react differently to the changes in the energy system.

We can feel clicking in the neck joints and in the jaw; the ears can feel as though you are in aeroplane on occasion, and there are all manner of strange, unusual, tingly and electric sensations to be noted throughout the whole body, from the tips of toes to the tips of your hair, as energy starts to move.

It also common in the course of many EFT treatments to yawn, and to start to feel spacey, very relaxed and tired. This usually happens around the Zero Point of Nothing and it is important to continue with the next round of EFT to get beyond that into positive energy flow, out of the fog and into the sunlight, as it were.

An interesting phenomenon in some EFT treatments is tearing of the eyes, which feels quite different to ordinary crying. Sometimes, one eye alone can cry whilst the other remains entirely dry. This can feel very strange but makes perfect sense if the problem blockage was situated on one side of the energy body but not the other.

Crying is also something that can happen during an EFT session. Please do not be afraid of it or distraught by it. It is a physical response to a major pressure release and a good thing. Keep breathing deeply and keep tapping; soon, the tears will literally "flow away" and you'll feel clearer, calmer and brighter, refreshed like a landscape after a thunderstorm.

Starting to chuckle or laugh is also a direct response to energy movements. This happens spontaneously when energy flow increases quickly; but that's always something that tends to happen around the +4 region of the SUE scale. Laughing is wonderful, but by all means, tap the energy flow even higher so you literally start to glow.

Emotions can rise up in great waves of feelings for which no words suffice. This is only energy in motion and once again, nothing to be afraid of. We are accustomed to try and hold these kinds of feelings back, down and in; when you are treating yourself with EFT, simply let these waves flow as you keep tapping, breathe deeply. Focus on, "This is only an energy!" If the energy can flow unhindered through you and out, even the most intense emotions can be gone in seconds or flash through even quicker than that.

This takes us to the observation that it can be quite shocking to find that an emotion which has plagued us perhaps for decades can be "gone in a flash," so easily, so readily.

Every person who learns EFT has to come to terms with that in their own way. We can tap on, "If this is so easy, why did I have to suffer so much? Why did no-one tell me this?" and find our own resolution, our own Healing Event on the topic, our own understanding of our experiences and our lives.

All these experiences, the Healing Events and many more are a part of the EFT experience as each one of us starts to learn about ourselves in a new way.

The main thing is:

Don't be afraid.

"Afraid" is an energy blockage. It is only an energy, and nothing more. There is nothing to be ashamed of, nothing to be afraid of. When there are energy blockages causing stress, people will naturally think all kinds of irrational thoughts and worry about all manner of things which are entirely irrational.

"I'm afraid that if I tap my pain away, I'll have nothing left ..."

"I'm afraid if I think of that, the emotion will be so unbearable, I'll go insane ..."

"I'm afraid to lose control ..."

"I'm afraid that my wife wouldn't love me any more if I was too perfect ..."

"I'm afraid I'll get addicted to joy and pleasure if I tap my SUE rating up too high ..."

"I'm afraid if I tap my guilt and shame away I'll start behaving badly ..."

60

"I'm afraid if I tap on that problem, it'll be solved and then I won't know what to do ..."

"I'm afraid if I tap on the problem, it won't be solved and then I won't know what to do ..."

"I'm afraid if I empower myself too much, I'll walk out of my marriage and then what will become of my children ..."

"I'm afraid of what I might find out about myself ..."

All these kinds of fears and many more besides are simply energy blockages that cause fear and stress, and we are always better off without them, in mind, body and spirit.

The most transformational aspect of the EFT experience is that we really do not have to be afraid any longer. We can treat ourselves for the fear, remove the blockages and what we're left with will be reality, and the truth about the situation.

- **This is an extraordinary thing; being able to stop being afraid is probably the greatest gift of all.**

In fact, using all our fears as a diagnostic to let us know it's time to re-energize is the perfect place to be.

Energize Your Life!

When we first started out with EFT, we only thought in terms of "tapping our problems away."

This was understandable as up to that point, there was nothing like EFT available, and we all had so many problems we wanted to "tap away," we were immensely grateful to just find some minor relief from our most pressing problems.

We didn't realise at the time that in energy work, Zero really does mean Zero - nothing.

Feeling nothing is not a good place for the energy system to be. It is a kind of no-man's land of neither here, nor there; and although obviously it feels much better than to be in pain, feeling nothing is not the solution to our problems.

We learned eventually that in order to work with EFT correctly as a modern energy modality, we need to go much further, and experience the opposite of the original bad emotions in order to be sure that the problem is really cured.

We create set ups to describe our problems so we can tap them away; and that's where we start.

When we get to or around the Zero Point Of Nothing, we have to start thinking in a different way.

- **Now, it is no longer about what we don't want any longer, but what we do want instead.**

For example, if we start out with, "I'm feeling really sad" at -8 on the SUE scale, and after some rounds of EFT we have arrived at the Zero Point Of Nothing and now feel sadness no longer, we need to switch into thinking, "OK, so now I'm not sad any longer - how would I like to feel?"

The answer to that question gives us our first positive set up, in this case, "I want to feel that life is worth living," with the reminder phrase of, "Life is worth living!"

After this round, the person rated themselves at a +4 and said they felt really quite happy and inspired - and were ready to call it day, say, "Well, that was great! Thank you very much! Not only am I not sad any longer, I actually feel fine! Wow!"

- **But +4 is not anywhere near +10, and the healing event has not yet happened.**

"Quite happy," "pleasantly relaxed," "fairly cheerful," and "feeling fine" is OK - but we can go beyond OK, and in fact we must go beyond that if we don't want to feel that same sadness again soon enough.

The original sadness was at a -8, so it stands to reason that our Healing Event must likewise be found at +8 or preferably above that so we can be sure the original sadness will never, ever come back.

As it is literally unheard of in healing and therapy that you can "make sadness go away" just like that and experience peace, never mind starting to feel fine, it is understandable that people stop too soon and walk away too soon, without having claimed that awesome gift that is waiting on the positive wing of the SUE scale - the real Healing Event.

We encourage our person who is feeling fine to stop and think for a moment - the last set up was, "Life is worth living!" This is great, but can you allow yourself to want even more than that?

If there were no limits at all, what would you like to feel?

The person thought about it and then said, "I would like to feel fully alive." That became the set up, with, "Fully alive!" the reminder phrase; and halfway through that round of EFT, the person jumped up and started laughing in delight - the Healing Event had happened, they felt electric, full of energy, and had to express this by dancing around the room.

When asked what they thought in hindsight of having missed out on that experience by walking away too soon and taking the +4 as the best you can get, this person cried out, "That would have been awful! I've never felt like this before, I didn't even know I could feel so alive! This has changed everything for me - I feel like a whole new person!"

The Healing Events and the high energy states at the +10 end of the SUE scale really do that, they create a whole new energy body that is different than it was before. The new energy person is stronger, has had a big problem solved and feels better than ever before.

- These experiences of the Healing Events and high energy flow also change the future.

Now, this person has personal knowledge that they don't have to be sad and can change that into feeling hugely empowered in a short period of time.

This affects how they think and feel about all their problems; has taught them a super important lesson about the reality of energy flow they will never, ever forget, and the next time this person does EFT, even that will be a different experience altogether.

Thinking about how you want to feel and tapping for that is not just important when we deal with specific problems and emotions we want to "tap away."

- **At any time, anywhere you don't feel quite right, you can ask that question of, "How would I like to feel, right now?" and use the answer for an energizing EFT treatment.**

Allow yourself to want more and more as your energy flow climbs higher and higher on the SUE scale. Our energy bodies really are designed to feel that good; there is nothing artificial about improving the flow of energy. We can even say that living in high energy states is our birthright.

By focusing on what we want to feel, and learning to make that turn beyond mere pain cessation into the positives, we can start to get what we all want out of life - at the end of the day, it is all about feeling, feeling good, feeling better, and feeling better still.

In the following section, we are going to learn some basic EFT protocols which can be very helpful to find the best possible set ups for you.

Part 3 - The EFT Protocols

Different Protocols For Different Problems

The EFT round stays always the same; we direct the effects of the treatment by tuning on on the problem.

This can be done in a number of different ways.

In the last chapter, we have discussed how you can simply start with a description of the problem, and how to be specific enough to create a good set up.

In this section, we are going to discover a range of EFT treatment protocols to work with different kinds of problems in various ways for elegant and successful, easy EFT treatments.

The EFT Story Protocol

The first and easiest way to deal with a problem that has a story is to use the EFT Story Protocol.

Here, we simply tell the story of the problem, and as soon as we notice any sign of stress, we stop and tap on the last thing that was said.

For example, here is a person starting to tell the story of their traffic accident.

"I was driving down the motorway on my way home, just like I'd done a million times, and it was dark and raining hard."

At this point, the person started to become stressed and uncomfortable. We can see that easily from the outside, as they frown, rub their hands together, their breathing is getting faster and they're starting to sweat.

 When we do the EFT Story Protocol by ourselves in self help, we have to become aware of these signs of stress from the inside.

This is not at all difficult; just pay attention to your own feelings, the sound of your voice as you tell the story out aloud, your own breathing and what your hands are doing to really notice when you start getting stressed as you tell the story of a problem.

In the example, the gentleman who had the traffic accident stopped there and his first EFT set up was the last words he said before he got really stressed - "It was dark and raining hard," with "Dark & raining hard" as the reminder phrase.

We start the story again from the beginning to check if the "dark & raining hard" stress has been relieved, and it has, because the person now continues on with the story, "I was driving home, it was dark and raining hard and I was very tired, my eyes were burning ..."

Here, the stress is back, so he tapped on, "Very tired and my eyes were burning," as the set up and "burning eyes" as the reminder phrase.

So the story continues, and every time there is a stress spike, we simply stop and treat it, thus building a path to the heart of the problem, step by step, taking out stress and fear as we go along.

By the time this gentleman got to the main event, "I woke up with horrible start and there were the blinding lights of the truck right in front of me and I knew I was going to die," he was quite calm and even the memory of the head on collision which had left him paralysed was now manageable.

 It is the step by step stress release in the story protocol that we get the energy system "ready" and strong enough to face the main event, the near death experience in this case, and release the huge amount of energy that was stuck since then.

This is a very useful, global EFT protocol that is also very safe and supportive, really building that all important stress free path towards the very highly charged memories and energy system events.

By going through the story very methodically and tapping on all and every stress we can find, we really resolve the whole problem group which is often more than "just" the head on collision.

An important note: Don't be in a hurry to get to the heart of the problem. Take your time and de-stress properly, re-energize properly before moving on. A few more rounds of EFT won't matter and it will be much easier to deal with the heart of the problem when you get there.

You can use the EFT Story Protocol for memories, and for every kind of problem that can be told as a story which has a beginning, a middle and an end in that order.

As long as you de-stress properly along the way, take your time and not move on any faster than feels absolutely comfortable, you'll be able to release the energy blockages caused by the events in the story successfully and reliably.

The EFT Body Protocol

For some problems, we don't have a clear memory or a story.

These include strong feelings and we don't know where they came from; feelings from events so long ago that we can't be sure what the story may have been; repeating emotions that we don't know how we got to have them, and problems you simply can't put into words at all.

In the past, people used to think that having powerful, uncontrollable emotions meant you were crazy; now we know that these are movements of energy through the energy system that are running into blockages and causing physical pain and discomfort through the 6th sense, the feelings in the body which have no physical origin.

- **The EFT Body Protocol works by making very specific set ups out of physical sensations.**

Rather than saying, "I get so angry," for example, we would focus on the feelings in the body and ask, "Where and how do you feel that anger in your body? Show me with your hands."

The answer might be, "It's right here (rubs chest) like a fast, hot rush right through the centre of my chest."

We tap with the set up of, "Fast, hot rush through the centre of my chest," with the reminder of, "Hot rush."

A tip: When working with the EFT Body Protocol and actual physical body sensations, put the free hand on where the feeling is located. That helps the process of improving energy flow along.

We can use the EFT Body Protocol in many different ways.

For example, if there is an ongoing problem that might have many, many potential set ups, as you would find in an old marriage for example, we can just ask, "When you think about your marriage, where do you feel that in your body? Show me with your hands."

This will take us to the most important, most pressing, most disturbing energy blockage relating to that marriage, without ever having to talk about who did what to whom, when, why, or how often.

This is a very direct and powerful approach to using EFT which brings about likewise, profound changes in the way a person feels.

When you use the Body Protocol, make sure that the energy blockage and the sensations in the body related to this have moved all the way through and out.

Then we can go on to the positive wing and tap for good feelings in relationship to this marriage and bring about a massive shift in the way the person thinks and feels about their situation.

The EFT Body Protocol is also very useful for people who don't like to talk about emotions, or who can't talk about emotions, such as young children.

Everyone from a young age can show where their tummy hurts when daddy says mean things, for example; and by not having to worry about what it all means, or going on a lengthy old fashioned Freudian style trip through the ins and outs of a problem, we can make healing changes fast, easy and reliable - even for old problems where there are no memories to guide us and only the feelings now remain.

The EFT Body Protocol can also be used in "Secret Therapy," meaning that we don't have to talk about any specifics, do not have to re-live memories of any kind and nobody has to know what the problem is or where it came from. This is an amazing gift in many ways and opens the door for finding healing and release from problems which in the past caused many to have to suffer in silence.

Finally, the EFT Body Protocol is the obvious choice for using EFT in the treatment of pain and psychosomatic pain, or painful symptoms of illness.

The Mindful EFT Protocol

This is an interesting protocol, especially for self help, in which we don't speak a set up at all but instead use an object, artefact or any external stimulus to focus on.

For example, a person who has an addiction to chocolate can place a favourite type of chocolate on a desk before them and simply "tune in on the chocolate" whilst going through the EFT protocol.

The protocol is called the Mindful Protocol because in the absence of having to think and speak, we can really focus on our body sensations, the flow of our thoughts and memories, our breathing, and how each treatment point reacts when we tap it.

For this protocol, you need to have something there you can focus on and which will in fact replace the spoken set up.

The focal object can be any kind of representation that reminds you of the problem.

It can be a photograph, a real object, a drawing, a symbol, or words written on a piece of paper.

The focal object can also be a place, or music, a memento, anything that will help us tune in to what we want to work with.

In many situations, and with many problems, using Mindful EFT can be quicker, more direct and more powerful than trying to find the right words.

For example, there was a lady who was very reversed to using computers, even though she had to use them for social and business purposes all the time. There were many reasons and many incidents of trauma relating to computers over many years; so instead of trying to name them all or even find one to get started, she simply sat in front of her (turned off computer) and started to tap the Mindful EFT protocol. After two rounds, she felt ready to switch it on, and it already felt different. She kept tapping rounds, and then it occurred to her to call up a word processing document. When she had tapped on that, "everything changed - all the fear was gone and I actually wanted to start writing something!"

Another example for using Mindful EFT was a lady whose husband of 45 years had recently died. There were so many emotions, thoughts and memories that it was very difficult to know where to start; so this lady sat with a photograph of her husband and tapped until she could feel at first some of the sadness recede, and later on, "I could feel my love for him coming back and that was wonderful, healing, an amazing experience."

A lady with a severe spider phobia got a friend of hers to write the word, "spider" on a piece of paper, then place the piece of paper face down on the far side of her sitting room, while she remained standing outside in the hallway, tapping herself whilst thinking in the direction of the spider paper in the other room.

When she felt ready, she entered the room and a few rounds later, the friend was able to turn over the paper so the word "spider" became revealed. Two more rounds and the lady expressed a desire to see a picture of a spider, something which had previously caused full blown panic attacks.

This last example is a good guide on how to treat even very negative reactions with the Mindful EFT protocol.

Start somewhere where you are comfortable and start to tap. Don't get any closer than you really feel you want to. Take all the time you need and do as many EFT treatment rounds as you need; this is not about overcoming fear but simply about releasing energy body stress so a stress free path towards the focus object comes into being - **naturally.**

There was a moment with the lady when she stood in the corridor when enough stress had been released and she *wanted* to go into the room where the paper was.

There was again a moment when she *wanted* to come closer; and another shift when she *wanted* to see the word and have the paper turned over. The final shift in that session happened when she *wanted* to see a picture of a real spider - that's the way to do this right.

The lady and her helpful friend went to a pet shop which had real live spiders for sale about a week later and they "danced in the street in delight" when the problem had gone.

Energy work is not psychology; it's a different modality. We always simply unblock blockages in the energy system and then improve the flow of energy through the energy body. This naturally leads to less stress, less fear and then that turning point into positive emotions which are the true healing for the problem.

The main point for the Mindful EFT Protocol is to focus directly on something that causes problems and then to take it step by step and not progress any faster than you really want to.

In that way, even very heavily emotionally charged encounters can be controlled and we can do one round of EFT after the other, building that stress free path to the heart of the problem, until it is solved.

The EFT FreeFlow Protocol

The EFT FreeFlow Protocol is a more advanced treatment to improve energy flow; its main feature is that instead of a single set up, we allow the set up to evolve from point to point.

This protocol is useful to investigate a problem that might not be very specific or clearly understood; and we can use it for removing general energy body stress on any given topic.

It is also a very interesting experience that engages mind, body and spirit and teaches us much about energy flow, thought, feelings, body sensations and can help us understand ourselves much better.

For example, here we have a person who knows they are upset but are unsure why, plus this has happened often in the past and they would like some forward movement on the whole thing, even though they don't know what the problem is.

The first set up, in the Heart Healing position, was, "Peter really winds me up!"

Instead of tapping a whole round on this set up, in EFT FreeFlow we let the point we're tapping on dictate what the set up will be. Whatever comes to mind when we tap on the point is going to be the phrase to tap on this point.

In our example, the person tapped on the top of their head and said spontaneously, "Peter is so stupid! He drives me crazy!"

We keep on tapping on the top of the head and breathing deeply in and out until we feel we want to move on to the next point.

We tap that and get the next evolving set up, which in the example was, "I just don't understand him, he's so alien to me."

The beginning of the eyebrow point resulted in, "I wish I had more patience ... with him ... just more patience ..."

The corner of the eye produced, "I don't suffer fools gladly," and under eye was, "They don't see what I see." The person tapped on that for quite a long time before sighing deeply and moving on to under the nose, which produced, "I'm scared of not understanding, I'm scared of being wrong." This became, "I'm scared," under the mouth, and evolved to "My father scared me," on the collarbone point. There were some intense body sensations, including stomach rumbling, heat in the head and neck, and quite a long time tapping on the collarbone until the person started to smile and moved on to the thumb point with, "No need to be scared," which evolved all the way to, "I feel really powerful," by the time they arrived at the Karate Chop point.

The final Heart Healing had the person say, "Only the strong can really love, now I know why I couldn't love Peter right before, and now I can, I feel such love for him, he is wonderful, he really is."

- Allowing the statement to evolve on every tapping point in direct response to the feelings, thoughts and memories tapping on that point evoked in the first place is an interesting and very powerful application of EFT.

It is worth bearing in mind that this is not psychology or psychotherapy in any shape or form but once again, simply energy work; the purpose of EFT FreeFlow is in its name, to get energy flowing powerfully and freely, by removing blocks to the energy system and using every one of the EFT treatment points and places to their maximum capacity.

The EFT Proxy Protocol

The EFT Proxy Protocol (also known as Surrogate Tapping) is to tap for or on behalf of someone else.

- This someone else can be another person, such as a child or a partner, friend, boss or colleague;

- It can be an entity such as a company, a family, team, band or group;

- It can be an animal, including companion animals, farm animals or wild animals;

- it can be an aspect of yourself from the past (who is no longer "you, now");

- and it can be an aspect from the future too.

EFT By Proxy is very simple and instead of saying in the set up, "I am afraid of spiders," we simply say, "Bob is afraid of spiders," if we're proxy tapping on behalf of Bob.

The EFT Proxy Protocol has a dual action.

The first is simple and direct; when we tap on behalf of someone or something we are worried about for whatever reason, of course we ourselves receive stress relief and improve our own energy flow.

The second action is something you will only find in energy work; namely that the target of your EFT Proxy treatment will change as well.

 We are much more connected on the energy levels than when we are walking around all separate from each other in physicality.

In EFT Proxy tapping, we are using these connections to make changes and improve the flow of energy.

There are many times and places where proxy tapping is an excellent path to take. From parents who worry about their children, to spouses who want to tap on something in their partners that upsets them; from grandparents tapping for the grandchildren far away to customers proxy tapping a company that is not treating them right; there are a thousand and one uses for this protocol.

A very interesting application of the EFT Proxy Protocol is to tap for past aspects and future aspects of the self.

Instead of saying, "When I was a baby, my mother abandoned me," we can proxy tap the past aspect (the baby that once was but isn't here any longer) by tapping on "the abandoned baby."

This works in effect by sending energy to those systems which still have "abandoned baby problems" today and targets the EFT treatment correctly.

It also makes it much easier to be compassionate and hold a real will to help the past aspects.

We can also use proxy tapping for future aspects, for example "the aspect of me who will have to give that scary presentation next Friday." We can tune in to the future aspect and tap for what will be bothering them, for example, "The aspect will be terrified to forget his words," as the set up with, "forgetting words" as the reminder phrase.

Proxy Tapping is a very important and beneficial part of EFT energy work that has many uses and will always make you, the one who is doing the Proxy Tapping, feel much better.

The Loving Touch EFT Protocol

There are times and places when we cannot physically tap on ourselves, or on another person. As EFT is energy work, and it is the healing hands of energy that make the changes in the energy body when we touch the EFT treatment points and places, we can do EFT without touching with the physical hands at all - and that is the Loving Touch EFT protocol.

In the Loving Touch protocol, we don't use a set up statement or a reminder phrase, we simply focus on "love" in the form of a loving touch.

Love is the most powerful and most healing energy form of all. It doesn't judge, doesn't exclude and just a little bit of love energy is wonderfully healing and empowering in all ways.

Now, consider for a moment that your healing hands of energy are not tied to your physical body and can freely move on their own accord.

Keeping your physical hands still and relaxed, let your hands of energy rise up and assume the Heart Healing position now.

Breathe deeply and easily and pay attention to the sensations in that area where your energy hands are touching your heart centre now. You can think or say "Loving Touch" on the out breath.

Take a deep breath and sense the top of your head being touched by a loving hand; take another deep breath as the loving hand moves down to touch the third eye point; and so on all through the EFT treatment round.

This is an excellent and very meditative protocol that gets better with practice; by all means, practice this each night before you go to sleep to re-balance your energy system with the loving hands of energy.

Please note: If you find it difficult to keep your focus, this is usually an indication that you are too stressed; try tapping a round or two of normal EFT first and then do the exercise again.

It is well worth learning to do this and a wonderful addition to the other EFT protocols; and when the time comes you really need to use this on yourself or on another person, you'll be glad of your practice and experience.

Highly recommended!

EFT Protocols Summation

Each one of the six major EFT Protocols:

- **The Story Protocol**
- **The Body Protocol**
- **The Mindful Protocol**
- **The FreeFlow Protocol**
- **The Proxy Protocol**
- **The Loving Touch Protocol**

... has many uses in the self treatment with EFT.

For practice, try each one of these protocols on a problem or situation that stresses you.

If in doubt, just start tapping for "Stress!" first of all, and go with the flow of the moment.

Personal experience is the best way to learn how these protocols work; and when a pressing real life problem comes your way, you'll know just which one to use.

Part 4 - The A-Z Of EFT

There is just so much you can do with EFT, the applications are truly limitless!

The reason for this is of course that **EFT is essentially a "content free" process** that can be applied anywhere any problem has an emotional component – and can you think of any kind of human problem that does not have an emotional component, or two, or three?

Beginners in EFT are sometimes astonished at the sheer simplicity of the actual EFT protocol and can't yet conceive of all the things you can do with it.

This next section is here to firstly discover the potential of this simple, content free technique.

Secondly, it is designed to be a teaching set to learn the underlying concepts through using EFT with a wide variety of people and a huge variety of problems. Each one of the sections is a piece for your learning and understanding of the technique and how to apply it with real problems; some aspects are highlighted from different angles because they are central and important, and each case story has something relevant to contribute to the understanding of the EFT process and how to use it to create change, healing and success.

We would therefore suggest that you read each section, even though at first glance it might not apply to you personally.

So now, here are some of the possible areas where you might like to apply EFT for yourself, your nearest and dearest, and/or your clients.

Remember our motto:

"Try EFT on EVERYTHING!"

EFT & Addictions

When we talk about addictions, we mean addictions in a structural and wide sense.

This is not just about addictions to substances such as heroin, cocaine, nicotine, alcohol, chocolate etc.; but all addictions.

What is an addiction?

An addiction is to use something to relieve stress which isn't a solution to the underlying stress problems.

For example, a particular person may experience stress and always responds to this by buying (yet another) pair of shoes.

Although the addictive action relieves the stress for a short time, shoes can't fix what's "really wrong" and so the stress comes back, and more shoes will be bought.

Addictions arise when a person who is very stressed experiences stress relief from something and has a Guiding Star experience - "This is the answer to my prayers, this is the solution to my problems, I'm saved!"

Once this happens, the person can't help but "default back" to that which gave them momentary relief for their severe stress, every time stress becomes very high again.

When we address any type of addiction from the energy angle with EFT, we can choose a number of different "entrance points" to the problem system in order to achieve true "emotional freedom" at last.

- **The first and most important step to treating addictions with EFT is to reduce stress.**

Every single person who has become addicted to something has underlying stress problems. Their general stress levels had to have been much higher than normal to make them vulnerable to the process of addiction in the first place; this is always true and there are no exceptions.

Even with chemically highly addictive substances such as crack cocaine, a person must have been in a particular state of mind, body and spirit to even contemplate "trying this."

So the first order of the day is to reduce stress overall and before we even begin to try and convince a person that there is indeed, life beyond addiction, and that being free from the addiction is even a possibility.

We can start with general stress set ups, such as, "I'm very stressed," or "I'm unhappy," to take off some of the top level disturbances in the energy system, calm it down, and start to get some positive energy flow going.

 For all addiction treatments, it is extremely important that a person should learn to monitor their own stress levels at all times and immediately take action when stress levels start to rise.

To begin with, doing at least four rounds of EFT for "stress" every day, first thing after waking up and starting to think of the day ahead, at lunchtime, at dinner time, and before going to sleep at night, regularly, every day so it becomes a practised pattern, is of the essence.

We also recommend using the Heart Healing position often and immediately when stress levels rise too high. That takes only moments, and the three deep breaths plus the strengthening of the heart centre (the nuclear power generator at the heart of the whole energy system) helps to keep stable and lowers stress levels significantly.

This is the baseline treatment for all addictions and it lays the groundwork for more specific interventions with EFT.

Once the baseline stress comes down a little and the person has learned how to do EFT, we can treat more specific aspects of the addiction.

Treating The Object Of Addiction With Mindful EFT

An addict has a long standing and very complex relationship with the object of addiction, whether that is a behaviour such as sex, a substance, an object or a fetish, or even a person.

If we tried to put that relationship into words, we would generate endless set ups; not only that, but many strands to that relationship are outside of conscious awareness and a person wouldn't even know what to say.

By using the Mindful EFT Protocol directly, we create a short cut and in energy work, this is very direct and powerful.

We can bring the object of addiction to us, place it on a table before us, and simply focus on it as we do our treatment rounds of EFT.

If that isn't an option, we can write the name of the object of addiction on a piece of paper to help us focus on it.

The main purpose of engaging with the object of addiction in this way is to do EFT to release energy blockages and to improve the flow of energy, with as many rounds as it takes, until we are on a high positive reading on the SUE scale - +7 or above.

This changes the energetic relationships with the object of addiction at a deep and profound level; and together with ongoing stress relief, is foundational to the treatment of addictions with EFT.

Treating The Guiding Star With EFT

The next big leverage point to solve addiction problems is to deal with the Guiding Star, the original experience when the person structurally and absolutely "fell in love" with the addictive substance.

Even with long standing addictions that may have "crept up" on a person over time, for example in alcoholism, there is always one specific memory which stands out and where a person "learned" that the substance can help them feel better.

- **Every serious long standing addiction has a Guiding Star which holds the addiction in place.**

A Guiding Star is an energy system blockage just the same as a serious trauma experience, and it needs to be evolved for the person to get free of the Guiding Star.

Ask the following question: "When and where did it happen that you fell in love with X? Tell the story."

When we have the story of the Guiding Star experience, we can treat it with the EFT Story Protocol, step by step, until the person feels real emotional freedom and the energy system has evolved beyond the Guiding Star.

Here is an example.

This lady, let's call her Jen, has a long standing addiction to speed or amphetamines.

When asked where and when the moment happened that she fell in love with amphetamines, she told the following story.

"I was at a party, I didn't know anyone, the person who invited me to meet them there never showed up. I was thinking about leaving when this one girl said I've got something to get this party started, and she put this white powder into a bowl and then poured some bottles of sparkling wine and vodka on it.

"I didn't really want anything to do with it but because I was nearest the door, I got the first plastic cup with the stuff and everyone was looking at me, so I drank it.

"It didn't do anything at first but a bit later, all of a sudden the room lit up, rushed away at the sides and I felt, like I was alive for the first time in my life. I had such a good time, I was the life and soul of the party that night."

The moment the Guiding Star happened in her mind/body/spirit system was when the room seemed to rush away, and her conscious metacomment of "I am alive!" was the conclusion she drew from the experience.

All this is simply true; it happened and structurally, we cannot blame a person for wanting to feel alive (again).

As in all addictions, in this case amphetamines, vodka and sparkling wine cannot provide this feeling of aliveness long term; only a fully functional, freely flowing energy system can, but people don't know this unfortunately and so addictions are born.

The important point about working on Guiding Stars with EFT is that Jen needs to experience the truth of "being alive." To ask her to give up her quest for "being alive" is something that can't be asked of a person, and that's why addictions are so hard to let go of.

The Guiding Star moment represents a powerful, positive experience and it is very difficult if not impossible to make a person "not want to feel alive ever again."

Unless the Guiding Star is freed up and treated, whenever Jen needs to feel alive again, she structurally will turn towards the substance/s to help her in a moment of need.

In this case, Jen went through the story protocol, step by step.

There were many insights along the way, including how awkward she had felt as a teenager, how she had always felt out of place and disconnected from everyone and everything, how stressed and insecure she had been and how vulnerable she had been, particularly on that night when the friend she was supposed to meet never showed up and "abandoned her amidst a sea of strangers."

The real Healing Event happened when she tapped on "I want to feel alive!" with the reminder phrase of, "Alive," which changed half way through the round to an exclamation of, "I'm alive!!!"

Jen was so joyous and filled with energy, she literally danced around the room with excitement.

The EFT practitioner asked her later on what she would want to do if she needed to feel alive, and was offered a choice of amphetamines or a round of EFT, and she laughed and said, "You've got to be kidding me! That's not a choice, that's a no brainer!"

In all addictions, treating the Guiding Star experience to the point that a Healing Event comes into being which quite literally, "overpowers" the old

Guiding Star, is structurally of the essence. Without this essential treatment, a person is not in a position, no matter how much "will power" they might try to apply, to really get "beyond the addiction," once and for all.

Treating Addictive Cravings With EFT

The experience of addictive cravings can be significantly changed by applying the EFT Body Protocol.

"Cravings" are intense body sensations. By focusing on where we can feel the craving in the body, and using that as the set up, for example, "This shaking in my hands," or, "The churning in my stomach," we can direct the re-energizing effects of EFT to the place where it is needed the most.

It is helpful to become aware of the first signs of cravings, which may in the past have been ignored, and tap as soon as possible.

With all EFT treatments but particularly with addictive cravings, it is really important to bring up the energy flow so the energy feels "full" and fully satisfied, fully happy.

This makes the physical components of the craving easier to deal with and the overall experience much less stressful and painful.

Many addicts are used to having been locked in an endless battle trying to hold out against strong cravings with will power and have trained themselves to ignore the lower level signs, when it first starts.

Paying attention to the cravings and to treat them with EFT as soon as possible can break that deadlock and help a person understand the processes of their own addiction much better.

Treating Physical Withdrawal Symptoms With EFT

Physical withdrawal symptoms can be very severe, depending on the substances involved. When we address the emotions and energy body stress and improve the flow of energy, we may not be able to make withdrawal symptoms disappear, but we certainly can help stabilise the person, have them be less stressed, less afraid, and be able to move through the processes of physical withdrawal easier.

This is not to be underestimated; any situation, no matter how dire, if we can face it without becoming too stressed and terrified, is easier to deal with.

Giving a person time to learn EFT, to apply to stress, to learn to trust in it before the real withdrawal phase is being entered into also creates a different withdrawal path; the person feels stronger in mind, body and spirit and is a much better place to face physical symptoms of withdrawal because of that.

Treating The Reasons For Addictions With EFT

Finally, we can discuss what was happening in the person's life which made them vulnerable to addiction in the first place.

What kind of stress or pain is the addiction designed to relieve or save the person from above all else?

It helps to go back in time and think about the life of the person just before they made contact with the object of addiction for the first time.

What were their major problems, their main sources of stress, pain and fear *at that time*?

Those original problems were only postponed by the addiction; and the problems with the addiction itself then took over and took all the attention away from those original problems.

They remain unsolved to this day. In order to be able to move into an addiction free future and for a person to be able to trust in the fact that they will not become involved in another addiction, or fall back into their old patterns long term, these problems need to be addressed.

We are not talking about 20 years in talking therapy here; EFT is not psychology, it simply clears blockages in the energy system that were never known or addressed before.

When we go back in time to consider the circumstances of the person before the addiction got started, we talk in terms of a past aspect of the person.

In the example of Jen and her amphetamine addiction in order to feel alive, the person now is 29 years old and has been through a lot; the teenager who had the Guiding Star at the party was 16 and that is not the same person any more as Jen is today.

So we consider the teenager to be a past aspect of Jen, and we can ask Jen what problems the past aspect was suffering from which made her vulnerable to addiction.

This gives us and Jen a third party perspective, a new way of looking at old problems.

Jen thought about it and then said, "The aspect at the party was incredibly insecure. Always afraid. And that got started when her father left home, when she was 6. She felt afraid and alone ever since."

Using the EFT Proxy Protocol, Jen made the set up for, "The poor little girl felt so afraid and so lonely," with the reminder phrase of, "So afraid and so lonely." After this round, she reflected on the thought that the little girl had also always suspected that it was something she had said which had caused her father to go away. As a result, she had been very shy and not spoken to people "so she wouldn't say the wrong things."

This was a different kind of afraid for Jen so she made another set up for, "The poor little girl was so afraid," with the reminder phrase of "Afraid."

After this round, she started to breathe more deeply and said she felt that a weight had lifted, and she very much wanted the poor little girl to be happy, to have a happy childhood, to be carefree.

Jen tapped on "Carefree." At the end of this round she said how strange it was that everyone thought she was carefree because that's how she behaved on the amphetamines, just being able to go through life without a care in the world and just doing things without worrying.

The next set up, "Going through life without a care in the world," with the reminder phrase, "Without a care," made the shift to the positive side of the SUE scale. Jen said that she could see the little girl smiling at her and waving, running off to play and she felt much happier. Another round of EFT for, "Happiness," really made her feel "quite wonderful, I want to be happy, really happy, really enjoying life to the fullest and now I feel I can."

EFT & Addictions Summation

Although each one of the applications of EFT for addictions we've discussed is a pathway into the whole addiction problem system, addiction treatments work best when addressed in this order.

1. **Stress Treatments.** Of the essence to stabilise a person and give them the energy and power to successfully address all aspects of their addiction processes.

2. **Treating The Object Of Addiction With Mindful EFT**. This is the most foundational step in freeing a person from the many energetic entanglements and strands that bind them to the object of their addiction.

3. **Treating The Guiding Star With EFT.** The original Guiding Star experience with the object of addiction is the glue that holds the addiction together; when this has been treated, everything else will become much easier to deal with. This puts the person into the position of being able to say, "I don't want to do that any more, that's of the past, I want better than that now and this is my will."

4. **Treating Addictive Cravings With EFT**. For every day life, habitual aspects of an addiction and in the course of ending the addiction, this is extremely helpful and makes the experience of being able to not "resist" cravings but to experience something else altogether instead successful and motivational.

5. **Treating Physical Withdrawal Symptoms With EFT**. Having EFT as a well practised and trusted friend by one's side when physical withdrawal happens is priceless and can really help a person make it through this part of the process easier and much less traumatic.

6. **Treating The Reasons For Addictions With EFT**. This is the final step and perhaps the most important for the future beyond the addiction. All addicted people have had to be vulnerable and stressed in the first place; and even if this was decades ago, it is really important to finally address the problems which the addiction kept "on ice" since it began.

EFT & Affirmations

When EFT first appeared on the scene, many people became very confused and wondered if it was a good thing to tap on negative set ups, such as, "I'm afraid of flying."

They confused the EFT set ups and reminder phrases with affirmations, statements designed to create reality by basically "affirming" something that isn't here, isn't real at this time, and could be the exact opposite of the existing conditions.

For example, a person who has no money would spend time each day (often in front of a mirror) "affirming" "I am rich! I am rich!"

This would sometimes work but most of the time it didn't and nobody knew why.

When we take the energy body into consideration, this is easily explained.

When people have blockages in their energy system on certain topics, they will experience the corresponding negative emotions. This will naturally lead to such people not doing what they need to do in order to (get rich, get into a relationship, get healthy, etc. etc.).

No matter how much they wish and want, they are literally "blocked" and can't go there to get it, whatever it is.

When we tune into these blockages with EFT and take them out, we also remove the resistance to positive affirmations at the same time.

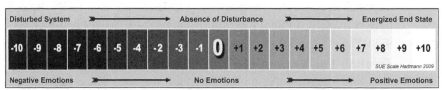

Problem Statements >>>>   naturally turn into >>>> Positive Affirmations when the energy flow increases.

Problem statements naturally turn into positive affirmations when the energy flow increases.

This is a natural process; nothing artificial is inserted, nothing artificial or untrue is added.

We start by "taking out the garbage" and when that's gone, the path is free to quite literally, choose to create our own destiny.

With the help of EFT that takes out the blockages to success, we are now in a position to create powerful positive affirmations that will really take hold and really do create reality.

Here is an example.

This gentleman has been trying to make the affirmation, "I am rich!" work for many years but it hasn't improved his financial situation which remains always precarious, always teetering on the edge of financial disaster, causing much stress and unhappiness, as you can imagine.

With EFT, we start with an honest assessment of what's wrong, what's blocking him, what is stopping him from succeeding and becoming rich.

So what's the problem? What is the big block to becoming rich?

Our gentleman, let's call him Jim, sighs sadly, shakes his head and says, "I don't know. I wish I knew what was wrong with me ... I've tried everything and nothing has worked ..."

The first set up was, "I've tried everything and nothing has worked," with the reminder phrase of, "Nothing has worked."

After this round, he sighed, relaxed a little bit and said with a wry little smile, "Well, I guess that was an over-exaggeration ... some things have worked but never enough to make a difference ..."

This created the next set up, "Never enough to make a difference," with the reminder phrase of, "Never enough ..."

After this round, he reflected that he had come from a family which likewise, always teetered on the edge of financial ruin, and there also had always been this sense of there never being enough of anything for anybody, all the time.

He said, "It's like we were living under a shadow, I'm living under this shadow still."

That was the next set up, "I'm living under a shadow," with "Living under a shadow," as the reminder phrase.

Half way through that round, Jim straightened up and took a deep breath. "I want this shadow to be gone," he said and finished the round, then started a new round with, "Living in the light."

At this point, his energy reading was on the other side of the SUE scale and he was smiling. "Can I really be rich?" he asked, and then did the next round on, "I can be rich," with the reminder phrase of, "Rich!"

As the energy flow improved visibly throughout this round, Jim started to glow and really smile, then laugh. He said, "Rich is so much better and means so much more than I ever thought before! It really is important to be rich, really rich, living a rich life filled with rich experiences, really living in the light, really living life to the fullest!"

This is a great example of how affirmations take on a whole new meaning and power when we add energy work; take out the garbage and then the path is clear to get new inspiration (literally!), new energy, new thoughts and ideas, and most of all, new and better feelings.

When Jim taps now for, "Rich!" this is going to energize him, reduce stress, and how can this not lead to a "richer life" for Jim in the long run?

You can replace Jim's "Rich!" with anything that you want in your life but that's lacking or not happening.

An excellent and really inspiring EFT pattern and application, highly recommended.

EFT & Anger

Anger is the one emotion which is held to be totally unacceptable in modern societies. It has been said that anger is just a version of fear, and that angry people are most of all, afraid of themselves.

When we work with energy, we can leave all the judgements behind and simply focus on the movements of energy through the body, and the structural repair work we have to do so that a person can have new and different experience.

The aim in treating anger with EFT is not "to never get angry again" but instead to allow the energies generated to move through as quickly as possibly, preferably in a lightning strike flash that lasts no longer than a hundredth of a second. This fast energy movement leaves a person clear, bright and very energized, ready for action - it is in fact the opposite of "blind rage."

Anger is also related to stress; but rather than just relieving stress, in anger problems we want to concentrate on "flow" when we tap, to keep the channels open and have a good, fast flow of energy in, through and out the energy body.

In people who have real anger management problems, there is one major blockage which stops the free flow of powerful energies. The energies build up behind the blockage and when the blockage finally gives way, we have an uncontrollable anger explosion over which the person has no control.

On the positive side, anger is a very physical emotion which reacts very well to the EFT Body Protocol.

We can feel the anger building up and can easily give a physical location - "Where do you feel the anger in your body? Show me with your hands."

Where we feel it is where the blockage is located; this is the blockage that has to be tapped away. The blockage is also located in a specific channel and it is important to trace that channel so we can know which pathway the energy travels on to leave the body. This is the pathway we need to keep flowing clear so when things happen in the environment, the channel is open and the energy can flash through and out quickly, without causing any of the symptoms normally associated with anger tantrums.

Here is an example. During arguments with his wife, Luca used to get very angry and eventually would "blow his top" and attack his wife physically. When asked to show with his hands where he could feel the anger building up, he put his hand on a place just above the stomach. When asked to tap on the blockage in the stomach, with the set up of, "This blockage in my stomach," and the reminder phrase, "This blockage," he expressed fear that if he removed the blockage, he would be angry all the time. He felt the blockage held every day anger in. The EFT practitioner pointed out that he had a lot of anger in the stomach, a lot of backed up energy in the stomach actually, and that this clearly needed to just flow out all the time. Luca thought about it and then said that made sense.

With the set up focusing on the blockage, a first round of EFT was tapped. Then Luca said that the blockage had moved up to his throat, and commented that he often felt words sticking in his throat and being unable to make a good argument verbally. The next round was tapped for the blockage in the throat and at the end of that, the sensation of the blockage had moved up into his head.

Clearly there was a channel here which ran straight up from the stomach to the throat and up into the head, with the last blockage right on the top of his head, where he would eventually "blow his top"!

The next round for the blockage on the top of the head, again with the reminder phrase of, "This blockage," brought the breakthrough and the Healing Event - Luca, who had been very tight and serious throughout jumped from his chair, started to laugh and said, "Oh that feels so good, I'm all electric, this is an awesome feeling!"

The EFT practitioner and Luca then practised keeping the channel open by the EFT practitioner speaking particular insults which in the past had caused Luca to "blow his top" - and they resulted in the same electric, good feeling.

Something else then happened in the session which is highly relevant to the treatment of people who have anger problems. Luca felt very guilty for things he had done in anger explosions in the past and wanted more EFT sessions to deal with that. There were also self concept problems expressed in such ideas as, "I must be a very bad person to be doing these bad things," "I have no control over myself and that terrifies me," and "I have no control over myself." These, although perfectly understandable, are also now only energy blockages and they too need to be removed so Luca can have a different experience with his emotions in the future, as will those who love him as well as innocent bystanders.

With a better understanding of how energy affects emotions, how energy blockages cause stress and an ongoing commitment to keep paying attention to energy flow, Luca felt he was finally moving in the right direction.

Proxy EFT For Anger

Anger energy management is something that can and should be learned from an early age. Many children suffer from severe anger tantrums and this can lead to all manner of problems down the line.

As with all anger energy management, by focusing simply on what happens in the energy system, we avoid making judgements that only make a person, young or old alike, feel even worse about themselves and get in the way of a successful relationship.

Explaining to a person how it works that they get these anger energies rising up, then they get blocked and finally explode and teaching them basic EFT for self help in the moment is something that should certainly be done, even if the person is only three or four years old.

If this causes difficulties, we can also use the EFT Proxy Protocol to tap on behalf of a person.

We can simply tap on "Luca's anger" which will bring some movement into the system. A more advanced version is to ask, "Where do I feel Luca's anger in my body?" and then tap by proxy until the energy can rise up, through and all the way out fast, creating that electric, exciting sensation as it goes.

Anger Energy Management For Everyone

It can be said that anger is mishandled energetically by everyone, not just those few people and children who so dramatically "blow their tops."

Because anger is deemed such an unacceptable bad, bad emotion, people everywhere try to not feel anger, and they push their anger down just the same as Luca was trying to do in the example.

People also like to believe that they don't get angry when in fact, they do.

A good starting point for changing one's relationship to the energy movement of anger is to do a round of EFT for, "It's ok to be angry!"

What we call anger is an energy form, a particular type of energy that can be very powerful and positive if it doesn't get stuck anywhere. A fast flash of anger energizes the whole system and gets it ready for some kind of action; this can be not just helpful but even life saving under many different circumstances.

Further, the fast flash through of this kind of energy feels very empowering. It could be said that people who habitually feel powerless, weak, hopeless and helpless are missing exactly that kind of energy movement which would set them alight, inspire them and potentially enlighten them even.

"Anger done well" in energetic terms might just be exactly what a human being needs to stand up to injustice, wrong doing and evil; to find the backbone and the energy required to do something about it.

There is also the matter of stored up anger over past injustices which has never been released. These energy forms which in some cases should have been released decades ago clog up and slow down the entire energy system and we are always better off without them.

Anger is a fascinating topic when we take the energy body into consideration. It is a cause of much human misery, in its expressed forms of hate, negativity and violence, as well as in its unexpressed forms of repressed anger. With energy work, we have a simple, clear path to evolve out of those unfortunate states of being when we take a completely different attitude to those energy flows, stop being terrified of them and instead, learn to handle them in a whole new way.

EFT & Animals

Animals too have energy bodies, and these energy bodies can suffer from the same problems and blockages as human energy bodies do. Also, these energy bodies make energetic relationships with our human energy bodies in much the same way we make these energetic relationships with other people.

This explains the extreme emotional attachment people can have with their companion animals. It can also be said that for certain people the energetic relationships with their companion animals and pets serve an important health function for the energy body, especially when there are blockages to human energy coming in. The energy of animals is on the whole very pure, very powerful, unshielded and in the case of companion animals, happily forthcoming but for the asking. Which also explains why when old or ill people are "allowed" visits from dogs, or are "allowed" to keep fish, birds or small mammals, they seem to come to life, and their mental, emotional and physical health seems to improve.

In fact, when we consider the relationships between people and animals from the energetic standpoint, so much more makes perfect sense. This includes why some people react to some animals with outright terror, and why an old lady might be adding more and more cats to her collection; and of course, it explains the severity of Animal Bereavement.

Animal Bereavement

In the past, many human orientated counsellors would dismiss people who suffered from extreme animal bereavement or pet bereavement, as it is also known. In line with the general societal idea of, "It's only an animal, not a person, so why are you making such a fuss?" people who suffered from animal bereavement found it difficult to be heard, to be understood, and to be given the wholehearted help they clearly deserve.

In modern energy work, we no longer make a distinction what may have caused a person to suffer with the symptoms of bereavement; we simply treat it, as soon as possible, to help the person feel better again.

Therefore, the treatment of animal bereavement with EFT is exactly the same as treating any other kind of bereavement, so please refer to the chapter on "EFT & Bereavement" for the treatment path.

Animal Behaviour Problems

It has long been debated amongst the scientific community "whether animals have emotions."

Anyone who has ever loved, lived with or worked with animals to any degree knows full well that animals have emotions.

As emotions are simply the expression of what is happening in the energy system, this once again makes perfect sense.

As with people, we want to make sure we are really dealing with a behaviour problem and not an underlying health problem, so please follow the same path as we would when treating a human being and have the animal examined by a veterinary surgeon. Again, as with people, many problems that express themselves in unusual or challenging behaviour and emotion can be caused by physical disease, which is not in our brief; once this has been excluded, we can address the problem with EFT.

The vast majority of animal behaviour problems are caused by just two factors.

The first is stress.

Animals respond to stress in the same way as human beings do, namely with an ever decreasing ability to deal reasonably, rationally and intelligently with their environment, the worse the stress becomes.

How much stress an individual animal can take before they start to throw temper tantrums and display extreme emotions, including autistic behaviours, withdrawals, anger outbursts, screaming fits, self mutilation etc. depends on their breeding to an extent, but more importantly, on their life's experiences.

Animals too can suffer from trauma to the energy system which creates serious malfunctions, and this reduces the amount of stress the system can cope with after it has happened.

For any presenting behaviour problem, and this is ever more urgent, the more severe it is, we need to de-stress the animal first of all. As animals in human care have no power over over their environment and thus cannot do many things we humans do to deal with mounting stress, such as being able to remove oneself from a stressful situation and using food, distractions and mental activities for example, the human caretakers have to do what they can to reduce environmental stress for the animal.

Then, we can use EFT to help stabilise the animal's energy system, and this has proven to be highly effective in practice.

In general, we don't tap on the animal but use the EFT Proxy Protocol to tap for the aspects of the animal which are showing the disturbed behaviours.

For example, Reega was a lovely dog, a cross-breed rescue that was intelligent and obedient. However, she would get very stressed when there were children around, especially noisy younger boys; and on one occasion, being prevented by the lead from running away, she snapped out and bit a boy who was skating on the pavement close by.

We may reasonably assume that Reega had experienced a traumatic event in which boys of that age group were involved; so the owner proxy tapped Reega for "Reega's fear of boys." As she went through the tapping round, she said, "I got a sense that it wasn't fear, it felt more like terror to me, an overwhelming terror." So for the next round, Reega's owner tapped on, "Reega's terror." At this point, she reported that the dog, who had been asleep in her basket in the kitchen, came into the room and curled up at her feet with a big sigh. The owner said, "I had this huge upswell of emotion, a huge sadness for the cruelty of people to animals, those cruel boys, whoever they were ..." So she tapped on "Cruel boys" which released a lot of energy, and halfway through the round, Reega lifted up her head and looked directly at her. "It was a magic moment," said her owner, "It was like something sparked between us, and she knew she didn't have to be afraid any longer, that I would protect her, that she could trust me with her life."

On their next outing, the owner took Reega towards a field in the park where young boys were playing football. "Before I tapped for Reega, she would have stared at them and started to tremble. This time, she just glanced at them and looked up at me instead, and even the end of her tail was wagging a little bit. I smiled at her, I felt such love for her, and then I took her over to the other side of the park to play with her ball."

For anyone who loves animals and feels a connection to them, using EFT with animals is an extraordinary adventure, and an amazing experience. Animals can't lie and they can't pretend something has happened when in fact it hasn't; when an animal changes its behaviour right in front of your eyes because you have done nothing other than tap EFT, it is difficult to continue to deny the actual reality of energy work.

By understanding that animals really do have emotions, and that these are based on the conditions in their own energy bodies, we can help animals live much happier, much more stress free and love filled lives.

At the beginning, we noted that there are two major components which influence animal behaviour at the energetic level. The first was stress, and the second is energy flow - or what is commonly known as attention.

Attention Seeking Behaviour Disorders

Animals are much more aware of the energy conditions around them and in their own bodies than we human beings are. An animal will notice right away when it falls short of interactive energy - the kind of energy that is exchanged between members of a species and which naturally binds a group of animals together. This could be a pack of wolves; a society of feral cats; a pride of lions or a herd of horses, a flock of birds, a swarm of fish and so forth.

When we take animals and isolate them away from what would be their natural companionship and the energetic strands that feed them with energy for life, information, and support, we create a shortcoming of these energies. The animal will naturally seek this energy from others in the environment; and in a companion animal/owner relationship, the owner is the first stop for providing this much needed social energy.

There is a poverty line for each individual animal within any given species of social interaction. When the incoming energies fall below that poverty line, behaviour problems must occur; this is simply a structural reality.

Unfortunately, we humans have been trained to withhold attention, especially when it is being directly asked for; we call the attempts of some animal (or a child, or a person) to gain this life energy they need "attention seeking behaviour" and think that's a bad thing, and we should punish it by ignoring the culprit, so they "learn to go without."

If we consider the structural needs of the energy body, this is a ridiculous notion; it is the same thing as telling an animal (or a child, or a person) to "go without" life giving food, or "go without" life giving water, or life saving warmth in a snow storm.

The more social the species of the animal in question, the more life giving attention, social energy it needs not just to barely survive, but to thrive and to have a strong, healthy mind, body and spirit.

When we tune in on an animal in order to do Proxy EFT for it, we are giving the animal exactly that which has been in such short supply - direct, powerful attention energy. This feeds and strengthens the animal's systems, makes it more resistant to stress, more resistant to disease and much, much more relaxed, logical, happy and communicative.

We deepen our energetic relationship with the animal when we proxy tap, and importantly, we open new channels of communication which stay open after the EFT sessions is over. This results in an improved relationship which brings benefits not just to the animal in question, but also to the person who did the tapping, and who now receives more social energy from the animal in return.

Animals & Owners

As the relationships between an animal and their owner are so strong, whatever is happening to the owner is also happening to the animal by default.

When the owner gets very stressed, of course their animals get stressed too; if this goes on for long enough, animals can and do develop behaviour problems and eventually health problems as well.

Animals also often show the problems of their owners by proxy; from the much quoted single older lady "whose poodle hates men," via the nervous lady with the "nervous cat," to the gentleman whose horse would bolt at the sound of a sports car engine and "he understood that, having been in a car crash that nearly cost me my life," of course animals take their cue as to what is what in the world, what needs to be loved and what needs to be feared, from their owners.

Many people consider animals as "angels," and in the case of proxy tapping companion animals for "their" problems, this is often quite practically true. The gentleman who nearly died in a car crash proxy tapped his horse for "freaking out at the sound of a roaring engine," and eventually discovered that this had been his own great trauma all along. He said, "If it hadn't been for my horse, I don't think I would ever gone there, or ever solved it. I am so grateful to Radar, he showed me what I needed all along."

Once his owner was free of the engine roaring problem, Radar soon calmed down and no longer feared sports cars any more.

Because of the intensive relationships between owners and their animals, all manner of relationship problems you would find in a mature and deep human-to-human relationship occur just the same. Owners may experience guilt, confusion; fear and worry in relationship to their animals and all of that gets in the way of a simple, free flowing love relationship that empowers both parties in a wonderful way.

In the past, we may have been confused about what is the animal's problem, and what is the owner's problem; when we proxy tap with EFT on any aspect of the relationship, we treat both at the same time, always and by default.

Animals & Health

No doctor can even repair a broken bone; the bone has to heal itself, and doctors try to provide the right conditions for this self healing to take place as best as it possibly can.

In the context of modern energy work, this is the same task for us when our animals become ill. We can't "heal" them per se; but we can do our best to provide the right condition under which self healing has the best chance to succeed.

When an animal is ill, of course the owner will be concerned, worried, scared and stressed.

As the owner is energetically the major part of "the animal's whole world," now "the world has become a stressful place" and that's not a good place to be in if we want to create a healing environment.

The first thing we want to do when the animal is ill is to treat our own emotions about this so we don't just become very calm, but actually energetically empowered, energized, to provide additional life giving energy to the animal's energy body at this time of need.

When we are fully energized, running on full power, as it were, now we can proxy tap for the symptoms, for the disease itself, for healing; and when we do that from an empowered and energized state, it is obviously much more effective.

As always, we cannot heal physical disease with EFT; but we can most certainly give our beloved animals the very best chance, the best environment to heal within.

Here is a story from a long time EFT user, Danny, and her cat, Gem.

"Gem was really getting on, she must have been about 16 years old. She used to jump up on the work surface to get her food because we also have a bunch of dogs, and she'd never get her food otherwise.

"On this one day, she missed her footing, scrambled and then got her leg stuck in one of the drawer handles under the worktop. I wasn't there when this happened but she was hanging upside down, screaming, and the dogs were barking like crazy.

"She was totally traumatized by this, and had broken her leg, and pulled her hip joint badly. When she came back from the vets, she was miserable, depressed, probably in a lot of pain and all the joy of life had gone out of her. As she was so old, I thought that would be the end of her.

"I felt really sorry for her and proxy tapped her for the shock and the trauma, for being in pain, for having lost her joy in life and she started to recover. I kept tapping for her. Then one day, all of a sudden I realised that I was still waiting for her to die, that I thought she was like an old lady who had broken her hip and we all know that's the beginning of the end, right?

"There was a huge, and I mean huge energy shift when I tapped on my belief around the little old ladies, and not a day later, Gem got up out of her basket by herself and started to hobble around the garden!

"That was a year ago and the leg has healed completely, she's happy, running around, no sign at all of going to her grave soon. I'm still amazed that me changing my mind about that little old lady with the broken hip had such an amazing effect on Gem. And I'm still wondering what effect that had on me ...!"

For many people, proxy tapping on their animals is the first real use for EFT they experience.

It is simply amazing what we can learn and how so many things can change, simply by unblocking our energy systems and that of our loved ones by proxy and improving energy flow.

For any animal, having an EFT enabled owner is good news indeed; and for the owners, we have a gift basket full of precious opportunities to evolve our relationships with our animals, help them more and have them be the angels to us that they were born to be.

EFT & Anxiety

The more destabilised the energy system becomes, the more we experience the effects in a direct progression.

Stress → Anxiety → Fear → Terror → Panic Attack

This progression can happen very fast, but the important thing is that it always starts with stress.

Everyone needs to understand how energy body stress destabilises mind, body and spirit and start to reverse stress to feelings of empowerment, energy and purpose; but people who suffer from anxiety and panic attacks need to really take this to heart, and in a big way.

The base level of every day stress needs to be reduced so that when something stressful happens (as of course it will in normal life!) the energy system "has somewhere left to go" and doesn't need to explode into a real panic attack.

People who suffer from anxiety are much more stressed even in a quiet room, all by themselves, in the absence of any danger whatsoever, than people who do not suffer from anxiety or panic attacks.

They do not realise however just how stressed they are all the time, because this has been going on for a long time and they have simply become used to feeling stressed, and ignoring those feelings, so they can get things done in the real world.

The longer this high baseline stress has been in operation, the more serious and significant the symptoms become, and they become ever worse over time.

The first thing we need to do is to de-stress, and that means removing blockages which cause energy body stress and to increase the flow of energy through the energy body.

Anxious people get very anxious at the thought of having even more energy flowing through them, as their experience is that there is already too much energy they can't contain and this is making them "nervous."

Too much energy in the system is only a problem when it is blocked somewhere and doesn't flow properly; when we release the blockages and energy flows freely, we do not feel shaky or trembling or jittery with energy, instead we feel happy, powerful, good.

Tapping on releasing and relieving "nervous energy," or just simply, "all my stress," "all my worries," "all my fears" can be a start to address the problems in the energy system of an anxious person.

We have a nice set up, called "The Freedom Spell" which can be used in anxiety problems. It goes:

"All of my (x) I now let you go, soften and flow, soften and flow!"

At X you can insert whatever troubles you, for example:

- All of my worries
- All of my thoughts
- All of my faults
- All of my fears
- All of doubts
- All of my confusion
- All of my stress ...

... I now let you go, soften and flow, soften and flow!

This is a good way to start to de-stress enough to get some ideas on what the problems are, what is causing the most stress right now, and to generally start self help treatments for anxiety.

A note: A good EFT practitioner can significantly help you improve your results. It is well worth doing a few sessions with a qualified EFT practitioner first to create a foundation for very successful long term self help treatments that can make high anxiety and the fear of panic attacks a thing of the past.

Once the top level of stress has been relieved to some extent, we can enquire into the original reasons for the energy system having become so destabilised in the first place.

Unless you were really "born this way" there has to be at least one event that was never addressed at the energy levels and which has significantly de-stabilised the energy system, thus making it vulnerable to stress in general.

EFT & Artefacts

Artefacts are objects which are no longer just material objects but have acquired an extra dimension because someone has a powerful relationship with the object.

All people make and own artefacts, the special things they choose to have in their environment for emotional reasons. With EFT, we can gain control over the artefacts in our lives, instead of artefacts controlling our lives.

The first and most obvious example of using EFT with artefacts is de-cluttering and hoarding.

People hoard certain types of objects because of an emotional response to the object. When we apply EFT to such objects, the energy bonds are broken and a person gets to experience "emotional freedom" from the artefact. Then they can make different choices and throw the artefacts away, sell them, organise them differently and generally gain control again.

For example, an older gentleman called Chester was hoarding old newspapers. His bungalow was filled from floor to ceiling with newspapers after over 20 years of hoarding them, leaving only tiny walkways now that were threatening to collapse in on him. However, the act of even thinking about throwing a newspaper away would cause him extreme panic, breathlessness, and the fear he would die of a heart attack.

An EFT practitioner went to his house to help him. After re-assuring Chester that he didn't have to do anything that would cause him pain, teaching him EFT and doing quite a few rounds simply to de-stress him and have him be comfortable with EFT and how it works, the practitioner asked him to focus on the newspapers and simply tap.

During the rounds that followed it was revealed that Chester had been looking after his parents. His father died; he was the reader of newspapers. After this, Chester started to put the newspapers by, unread and unopened, near the chair where his father used to sit. When quite a few had accumulated, his mother made him take them away; but then his mother also died. With no-one left now to tell him to clear away the papers, they had grown and grown over time. During one round, Chester tapped for "Father's papers," and realised that for all this time, he had never really accepted of dealt with his father's death, or gotten over the shock of finding his father dead when he went to bring him the morning papers. At the end of the treatment with EFT, Chester was able to call a removal company himself and have the papers taken away, to a recycling plant, and also started thinking about hobbies he used to have and very much enjoy before his father had died.

This is an extreme example of how a simple object such as a newspaper can turn into an artefact; however, the same principle is at work with all artefacts people choose to keep around, from photographs to wedding dresses, and from holiday mementos to jewellery.

Jennifer had a picture over her fire place of a sunset lake with a boat, painted in oils. She found the picture depressing but she had inherited it from her father and couldn't take it down. Tapping Mindful EFT on the picture helped her release the entanglement; Jennifer said, "I realised that I felt as though I was being disloyal to my father or not loving him any more if I took down the picture. It was his favourite, and I was his favourite.

"But now I know - feel - that he is in my heart and he would laugh at me and say, don't be silly, if you don't like it, sell it and put a happy kitten on your wall, it's your life, I love you and I want you to be happy."

Agnes, an older lady, had to move into a retired community and could not take her extensive collection of books with her. She was distraught and threatened to call off the move as she "would rather die with her books than live without them."

She tapped EFT with a practitioner on the phone whilst holding some of the books. During this, she found out that she had "the story of her life in books" on her shelves, starting from favourite books when she was a young child, to a teenager, to university and so on all the way to the current date.

Using EFT on each book herself over the next few days, Agnes was able to discover which books were the most important and precious to her, and which she could let go of, and so she ended up with a single box of her most beloved books for which there was plenty of space in her new accommodation.

Agnes said, "Before EFT, I felt books were my life. Now I know that my life is my life - and certain books are my good companions. It is lovely to be so clear on that, and I don't know how I could have made the move without knowing that."

As a final example, a lady called Trisha kept buying expensive handbags that she could not afford on her salary, and this had driven her deeper and deeper into credit card debt. When she tapped EFT on her handbag problem, she realised that it all came back to a time when a boyfriend had bought her an expensive bag, the first one, and the next day when she took it to work, all the other ladies in the office had crowded around and expressed admiration and jealousy. "I was the centre of attention, for the first time ever, and I felt so in love as well, I was glowing with happiness.

"Now I realise that handbags can't give me that feeling, only being in love can! I still like nice handbags but it's good to know what I'm really looking for in life, and now I won't accept substitutes any longer."

Artefacts are important reminders in our environment, portals to special moments in time that shaped our lives.

When we understand their true meaning, we can use EFT to make new and different decisions, and we always learn something important about ourselves in the process.

EFT & Aspects

In modern energy work, we sort out different "aspects[3]" of a situation, object, or a person by time.

No two aspects can be in the same place at the same time, and this simple observation resolves a lot of problems, including the so called "parts conflicts" as well as a veritable multitude of other conflicts and problems.

Aspects Of The Self

The Aspects Model of sorting through time is particularly useful when we are dealing with "aspects of the self."

We are used to using the term "I" when we think about "ourselves," but that can be extremely confusing, especially when we are dealing with aspects of ourselves who are way back in time, or forward in time.

"We" are not the same person today as we were last year, or ten years ago, or when we were 3 years old; to make this distinction between who we are now and who we were then, in energy work we refer to any self that isn't right here, right now, as "an aspect."

- **We talk about the aspect in the third person to make the distinction clear.**

For example, instead of saying, "I was five years old when I stole an apple," we say, "My five year old aspect stole an apple."

This five year old aspect still exists in the energy system but does not exist "in the real world" any longer; and by referring to that place in the energy system as "the aspect" we are targeting our set ups more logically and more directly, as "I" could be literally anywhere but actually, is only ever right here, right now.

This has many advantages.

First of all, if we remember something in the first person, and associate into that state from that time, we structurally "become" five years old again, re-live the entire memory from that standpoint once again, and really nothing is learned, and nothing is gained.

---

3   The Aspects Model, "Events Psychology" Hartmann 2009

This is particularly important when we're dealing with traumatic memories, as re-living the pain of the original experience yet again doesn't help us at all, it doesn't help the energy system in any way.

When we start to think, feel, talk about and tap for "that aspect who stepped on the landmine" instead, we gain clean and powerful leverage in EFT energy treatments.

There are many other advantages to working with aspects rather than endless confused "I's."

It is much easier to understand what went on when we consider the past events from our grown up perspective here and now; it is much easier to feel compassion to an aspect, to appreciate them and what they went through in a whole different way, and also, to love them.

We could say that it is structurally impossible to "love your self," in the same way we can't look back at ourselves with our own eyes, or jump over our own shadows; but we can certainly feel powerful love and compassion for a past aspect, or a future aspect.

This also leads to re-connection between aspects; and on the energy levels, this is very important to current well being, having access to one's own memories, and "feeling complete" as all the aspects together make up the life line and need to be energetically interacting with each other.

Talking about "yourself" in the third person may feel a little strange to begin with, but the many benefits outweigh this easily. Here is an example.

This young lady insisted that she "hated herself." This is the kind of global statement that causes chaos in the energy system and in and of itself, cannot ever be successfully resolved.

When asked what she had ever done to make this so, the young lady, let's call her Dee, said, "I can't forgive myself for going to that party that night, I was a total idiot. I deserve everything I got, and more, for being so stupid. That's why I hate myself."

When the aspects model was explained, Dee said instead, "I can't forgive the aspect, she was a total idiot, she should have been killed, that would have been the right punishment for her!"

One round of EFT with the set up of, "The aspect was a total idiot," with the reminder phrase of, "Idiot!" and Dee sighed and said, "OK, she wasn't an idiot. She was just young, didn't know anything really, and she trusted the wrong people. She was just naive ..."

When asked how thinking about the aspect was different than thinking about "I" and "me," Dee said, "I could see it from the outside for the first time, and there was no anger, just sadness, I felt sorry for the aspect, I've never felt sorry for myself, ever, not like that! It was such an eye opener ..."

110

That is not just a huge change of mind, but actually, a huge change of heart, which is far more precious.

The global rule is that the more intense the memory or topic you are dealing with, the more beneficial it is to use the aspect model and EFT Proxy Tapping to open new lines of communication, which are new lines of energy flow that were not there before.

Working with aspects we can also make excellent EFT interventions for future aspects.

For example, a gentleman we shall call Julius was extremely worried about a presentation he had to give to a tough crowd some weeks in the future. "It's going to be a nightmare, I have no idea what I'm going to do, what's going to happen ..."

Considering the future aspect instead of "himself," and wondering what we might do right here today to help that aspect in the future then, Julius said immediately, "He needs more confidence, more self belief."

He then proxy tapped his future aspect for confidence and self belief, and when he thought about the presentation again, he laughed and said, "It's funny, I can see him standing there, he has the mike, he has the floor, he has the power!"

Working with aspects is also very useful in the case of what seem to be conflicts. One thing can only happen at a time; so when there is conflict, what we really have is a sequential incongruency, meaning, one thing happens at one time, and another happens at another time.

Jame had "conflicts over being a too strict parent and a too lenient parent." As Jame can only be one of those at a time, we can tease that apart, sort it by time, and find out where and when it happens that Jame is too strict, and too lenient, and treat both aspects with EFT.

As it turned out, Jame was too strict when he was stressed; and too lenient when he was depressed. From the third party view point of thinking of the aspects, this was immediately obvious and resolved a conflict that had been going on for years with few rounds of EFT. Jame also came away from this with much more "self awareness" which happens when we think about aspects, one after the other, instead of a big muddled up "I" that has to be the most confusing of all concepts ever invented by human kind.

The final example of where thinking in terms of aspects rather than "me" is of good use is when it comes to considering who "I" really is.

"I" is the current representative of all the aspects that make up a person's life, and "I" is always only here and now.

This is a very empowering thought and place to be. It puts the power of decision into the present, where it belongs; it allows at least the potential of "you" and "me" making fresh, new choices if we wanted to.

We can forgive past aspects, love them, but we don't need to be bound by them.

Likewise, we can consider future aspects and wonder what "we" can do today to make their lives easier when it comes to it.

Sorting "our selves" through time is a nice easy, logical way to improve our energy work, create very powerful set ups and not have to re-experience bad memories all over again. It is an interesting shift in thinking and very useful indeed.

Aspects Of Problems

As is the case with aspects of the self, any aspect of any problem can only exist one at a time.

So even though it may seem that a problem has all these components and they're all tangled up like a big ball of string, when we sort problems by time, one aspect after the other, it makes it much easier to find good EFT set ups.

For example: "When I get upset, I just start to eat, I eat lots of chocolate, and then I feel angry at myself, but I can't stop buying more chocolate, and I like chocolate as well and I don't know what to do ..."

If we sort that out into a simple, linear time line of what happens, step by step:

- from buying the chocolate,
- to getting upset (when does that happen?),
- the whole process of struggling against chocolate
- and then the breakdown and the "giving in" to the cravings etc.

... we have a simple line of step by step events, one leading to the next, one after the other, and we can tap EFT to intervene in that progression at any stage.

You can create a time line simply by taking all the components of the problem, writing them down on separate pieces of paper, and then sorting them out by time: "What happens first? This or that?"

Doing this can by itself be very illuminating and useful; but what we also have is a list of set ups we can treat one after the other using the EFT Story Protocol.

A person who had a clown phobia was asked what they find particularly disturbing about the clown.

After sorting the list of disturbing clown qualities by time (What do you notice first? What is the next thing you notice? etc.) the aspects of the clown phobia were as follows, one after the other, sorted by time:

1. The big red nose
2. The weird eyes
3. The horrible mouth
4. The horrible hair
5. The horrible sounds it makes
6. The grabbing hands

The person tapped for one of these linear, sequential aspects after the other, each one representing what they noticed even though it was so fast normally that it was out of their conscious awareness, and there were lots of little shifts which culminated in the Healing Event in the middle of the round for "The grabbing hands."

That's when the person just started to laugh and exclaimed, "Clowns are so funny!"

It is possible that by sorting the aspects through time of what was particularly disturbing about the clown we re-traced the original sequence of events in the energy system which one after the other created these blockages, like a series of explosions being triggered one after the other.

Sorting By Time

The simple act of sorting aspects through time so we have an order and sequence of events is a great way to avoid confusion and find excellent EFT set ups that will likewise create excellent and healing changes in the energy system.

We can make sequential timelines of problems in our life, of events and their echoes, of behaviour patterns from start to finish that might take a month, or a day, or happen very fast. We can use this for goal setting by creating a sequence that has to occur to get us from point A to point B, and tap on every one until the path to the goal is entirely free and easy to reach.

Especially when we sort "our selves" into aspects by time, a huge amount of confusion is alleviated, and it becomes much easier to deal not just with the past, but also, with the future.

EFT & Beliefs

Our beliefs about the world, about each other and ourselves are based on personal experience. Beliefs are formed as the result of significant emotional experiences or events, as we call them, and to the person who holds the belief, the belief "feels right and true" because of that.

Beliefs can seem to be very illogical, damaging and limiting, sometimes downright insane, but if we take the events that caused beliefs into being into consideration, it is always logical how a person gets to believe what they believe.

For example, it is impossible for a person to believe that "all men are monsters" unless something happened to convince the person that this is the truth.

Changing beliefs with EFT can be a challenge because until we have changed the emotion or sensation relating to the belief, the belief is the truth to all intents and purposes.

A person may say, "Based on my life experiences, I have come to the conclusion that all men are monsters. I know this to be a fact, it is the truth, and there's nothing you can do to change my mind because it is the truth, you just don't know that because you didn't live through what I've lived through. If you had, you would know that I'm right, this is not a belief, it is simply the truth."

After many years of applying EFT to all kinds of beliefs, values and attitudes we have learned that there is a simple test to determine whether something is "just" a belief or the actual real truth.

Tap on it. If it goes away, then it wasn't the truth, just an energy blockage in your energy body. If it gets stronger, then it really is a truth, correct and valuable information about the world.

- **You cannot tap reality away with EFT.**

EFT only removes energy blockages; that is all it does.

It cannot change the facts of a situation; EFT only changes how we feel about these facts, therefore allowing us to interpret them differently.

We may say that EFT doesn't change our minds, but it allows us to have a change of heart instead; that is a powerful thing indeed and something that was rarely achieved with older methods.

114

Limiting Beliefs

Under the energy paradigm, a limiting belief is simply the conscious expression of an energy blockage, nothing more, and nothing less.

This is an extremely important concept to understand as limiting beliefs turn up all the time, and people have a tendency to try to argue with a person who holds that belief, has that energy blockage. From the outside, it often seems that person is crazy or stupid to believe what they do; until we really understand that they really cannot help thinking and feeling that whilst they have energy blockages in their system, we can't help them come to a new belief, a better, more reality based belief on the topic.

A classic example is a person who is very beautiful but is absolutely convinced that they are ugly.

All their bad feelings, thoughts and reactions on the topic are simply based on energy blockages in their systems; when we take them out, the person can look in the mirror and feel good about themselves instead.

Conversely, whilst they still have their emotionally painful energy blockages, if we tell them they are beautiful, all that happens is they will feel even more pain and have to reject that notion and even any talk on the topic absolutely.

Limiting beliefs that express the existence of very specific energy blockages are to be found everywhere, in every person, even in children already, and are being enacted all the time.

This is so all pervasive, it is even difficult to pick out examples because limiting beliefs, aka energy blockages, are endemic in societies that don't take care of their energy bodies and do not understand how to deal correctly with people and their emotions before, during and after important life events.

Here are some global topics to explore and to find limiting beliefs and their requisite energy blockages. You can use the SUE scale to determine the strength of your beliefs on these topic and then tap EFT to improve your SUE factor.

Health. How healthy are you? How strong? How resilient? How well does your immune system function? How quickly can you bounce back from illness and injury? What are your beliefs about health and age? What is healthy and what is unhealthy? What do you believe affects your health the most?

Wealth. How wealthy are you? How difficult is it to be wealthy? How hard do you have to work to be wealthy? What does it take to stay wealthy and grow more wealthy? What are your beliefs about money?

What are your beliefs about rich people? What do you believe affects your wealth the most?

Love. How loved are you? How lovable are you? How much love can a person give or receive? How easy or difficult is it to find true love? Do you believe in love? Does love hurt? How many soul mates can a person meet in a single life time? What do you believe affects your experience of love the most?

Spirituality. Does God exist? Is there life after death? Do you have guardian angels? How spiritual are you? What do you believe affects your spirituality the most?

People. What do feel about people? What are the best and worst kinds of relationships? What kinds of people don't you like? What is the truth about people? Can people ever really change? What are your feelings about humanity at large? What do you believe about people that affects your relationships the most?

Do please always remember that a limiting belief is simply an expression of an existing energy blockage, nothing more and nothing less.

This is true for yourself as well as for all other people; and as always, there is nothing to be gained by walking around with energy blockages in the system. This is a hindrance to real life, never a help.

To treat a limiting belief with EFT, we simply take the statement of the belief, "All men are monsters," for example, or, "I am ugly," or, "I was born poor and I will die poor," as the set up statement. At the end of each round of EFT, we check how the belief has evolved as more energy is flowing through the energy body and the feelings start to change. This causes a change in the words we use to describe the situation. As always, it is very important to keep tapping until energy flow is moving into the positive wing of the SUE scale - we are seeking a Healing Event that will express itself in a new belief that is more reality based instead.

Please remember also that "if it is really true, then you can't tap it away." EFT can't change reality, it doesn't change the facts, it only changes the way we feel about them - and that makes all the difference.

By learning to spot limiting beliefs and treating the energy blockages that cause them to be expressed with EFT as soon as possible, we can create wonderful, ecological changes in our lives.

Improving Beyond Belief

Something wonderful we discovered about working with EFT and beliefs happens when we don't tap on negative beliefs for a change but on positive beliefs instead.

For example, a lady tapped on her positive existing belief, "I am a good mother." You might need to have a personal experience of what happens when you tap on an already positive belief; this lady expressed it as follows.

"I knew I was a good mother and I was proud of myself because that's not an easy thing to be, day in, day out.

"When I tapped on it, there was this huge energy movement, like a giant wave that rushed through me and everything expanded, became bigger, wider - I had no idea how good a mother I'd been, there was so much more to it than I ever thought before!

"And it was like I was expanding into these new spaces, new opportunities, like ideas and ways to express my love for my children even more ... it was absolutely awesome! I'm still blown away thinking about it now!"

Energetically speaking, such a "huge wave of energy" will take out many little blockages as it goes; we can't predict which ones but it certainly feels that tapping on already positive beliefs can be much more powerful for personal evolution than tapping on many negative beliefs.

Making what's already working well even better can be a master key to personal development; so do take the time and think about your own best qualities, talents and abilities and shine them up with EFT for a truly unforgettable energy experience.

EFT & Bereavement

In the 1960s, a model was developed which is still being widely used today. It identified five stages of bereavement:

- Denial
- Anger
- Bargaining
- Depression
- Acceptance

What was observed there was an often very slow process with different forms of high emotions; when we think in terms of emotions as being energy movements we can feel, and take the energy paradigm into consideration, we can move through these stages of bereavement a great deal faster, more elegantly, and without getting stuck along the way.

What we have also found is that by using energy work, "acceptance" is not the last stage of grief.

The last stage of grief is when all the pain has gone, and instead, a person is left with nothing but love for the deceased. We call this stage "the immortal beloved" because a person who has healed of all their bereavement injuries really feels as though they are in love and will always be in love.

The final outcome of the bereavement process, the immortal beloved stage is the healed condition of bereavement. It is in energy flow terms a high positive emotion on the SUE Scale, +10 and this represents an advanced and evolved state of the human energy system.

There is another step in the bereavement flow which is missing from the old list, and that is the first state - shock.

The original shock of bereavement is a major event in the energy system, and when we wish to really heal bereavement related injuries in the energy system, this is the best place to start.

Any bereaved person will be very aware when they first heard the news, when they first became aware that the loved one had passed on.

First of all, we need to de-stress the bereaved person. When they are feeling calmer and more proactive, we can treat the bereavement shock with the EFT Story Protocol, step by step.

For example:

"I was at home, I don't remember what I was doing, tidying up perhaps. The phone rang and I just answered it as normal.

"For a moment, there was a silence and then I heard my mother's voice say, your father is dead.

"I can't describe what happened or how I felt, I just felt everything spinning, I wasn't sure what I'd heard, I didn't know where I was, everything fell to pieces ..."

With an event such as this, it really pays to tap every sentence fragment, one after the other, starting with, "I was at home," via "I can't describe how I was feeling," all the way to "Everything fell to pieces."

An important note: When we deal with powerful negative experiences and emotions such as in this case, we can often forget that this is energy work, and there really is a positive wing to the SUE scale.

It is really important to not stop at pain relief or "finding peace." The real healing happens when the energy flow increases to the point that the person can take a huge sigh of relief, begins to feel differently and starts to understand the whole event in a different light.

In the case of the lady who received the unexpected phone call a lot of energy was released; she cried when she tapped on the part in the story protocol when it came to "your father is dead."

At the end, she reflected that she had never felt safe in her own home ever since and could relate a lot of problems to this event which she had never realised before.

When the energy flow was improved further, by tapping the set up of "I love my father," with a reminder phrase of, "Love," she began to remember good memories for the first time in 20 years, since the phone call moment had happened. She also said that she now had a sense of her father's death not being the ultimate tragedy but more of a release, a spiritual ascendency experience, as he had been suffering with serious illness for a long time.

A further round of EFT caused her then to express tremendous gratitude for having had such a good father and that "I feel such pure love for him, just gratitude, it is so uplifting, I never knew I could feel like this."

By treating the first shock of bereavement with EFT, a new bereavement process comes into being. Different emotions and memories come along, but if we can stay focused on the fact that *this is a process*, and the more elegantly we can flow through this process, the sooner we will heal.

Throughout this new bereavement process, we can use EFT keep a flow to the process, so we don't get stuck with any emotion, be it anger, sadness, or depression.

The healed state of bereavement is love; to know this and to aim for this state of love and feeling loved, unconditionally and across time and space, makes EFT energy help for bereavement unique, priceless and precious.

Undiagnosed Bereavement

People experience the same process of bereavement not just when close friends or family members die; the bereavement process can also be set in motion when people leave, parents divorce, people move to a different part of the country, when children grow up and leave (the so called Empty Nest Syndrome which is absolute bereavement, pure and simple) and even when people change in significant ways to how they were before.

It goes further than this.

People can and do experience the bereavement process over pets, of course; and over losing a limb, losing skills or abilities due to sickness or old age for example; losing a home they have lived in for a long time, or generally losing anything that they had a deep and meaningful relationship with.

Children can experience full bereavement and show all the requisite symptoms when caretakers leave, or when a toy they have formed an intense relationship with is taken away or lost.

People also experience bereavement over changes in themselves, having the real experience and emotions as though an aspect of themselves has died when major life changes occur.

However a bereavement manifests, and whether we personally understand how someone could possibly start grieving over the loss of their hair, their youth, their garden or their favourite automobile, a bereavement is a real occurrence in the energy system and needs to be moved on into a bereavement flow as soon as possible.

Bereavement disturbances are very serious but when we apply the energy point of view and simple EFT treatments as and when required, without judgement or holding back, we can avoid major stress on the person which has been noted can turn to physical illness in the end.

Noticing signs of stress and disturbance and unblocking the energy system so it starts to flow brightly again creates a whole new bereavement flow and really helps people lead longer, healthier and happier lives.

EFT & Business

We await the day when the business world, which complains endlessly about how much working time and how much money is lost by stress in their employees, wakes up to the fact that in EFT we have a simple, profound, and practical solution to this problem.

Staff can be shown how to self treat for stress with EFT; and staff support can be taught how to assist others in releasing negative emotions, limiting beliefs, and all sorts of blocks to great and happy performance.

A humble telesales person, who could clear away at the end of a long day all the energetic effects of abuse, failure and pressure would be a different employee altogether after a week or two; of this we have no doubt.

Now multiply that by 20 million, and what effects would EFT have on the national economy?

People in business like to think that they're reasonable and rational; but all business is driven by emotion, from the creation of products and services to how the business relates to its customers and vice versa; from marketing to competition, and all the way through every human relationship that exists within any company.

Whether you are an employee, an entrepreneur, a manager or a CEO, EFT can absolutely transform every aspect of your day's work.

- EFT can give you extra energy so you can do more work in a shorter time and enjoy your work far more;
- EFT reduces stress you can think and work much smarter;
- EFT can clear the blockages to a free flow of new ideas;
- EFT can help you release traumas accrued in the business context;
- EFT can help you improve your relationships with the people you deal with;
- and EFT can raise the ceiling on what you might feel at this time is possible to achieve.

There are so many potential applications for EFT in business that the topic entirely exceeds the scope of the A - Z; here is a global work related pattern you can use to target areas where less blockages and more flow in your energy system would make the greatest difference.

Work & Play

- How do you feel about work in general? If the idea of "work" in and of itself doesn't excite you, it is time for EFT treatments. "Going to work against your will" every day is a sure fire way to getting ill in the long term, one way or the other.

- On the SUE scale, how much do you "like" the work you do? Can you improve the score, and how high can you take it?

- Within the global context of "your work," which aspects do you like the least? What stresses you the most? What do you procrastinate over the most? Whatever that is, if you treat it with EFT, you will be able to improve your "work happiness factor" and that always results in increased productivity.

- What do you enjoy the most about your work? Can you enjoy it even more? Using EFT to really improve energy flow for what you already like can really lift your overall energy levels.

- On your career path, what is the next step? How long/hard do you think it is going to be until you reach your next goal? What is standing in the way of progressing faster, easier, and having much more fun while you're getting there as well?

- Do you have a conflict between "work" and "play"? Is there a tension between what you have to do to earn money and what you love to do? Do a few rounds on "work and play" and release that tension, find out what happens when you do.

Global Business & Work Blocks

The biggest business problems as always stem from high energy events in the past that were never resolved properly.

These include business and work trauma including accidents and incidents at work; failed businesses in the past, having been fired from a job, having left a job because of traumatic experiences and so forth.

They also include "getting stuck" on highly positively charged events, such as winning a prize, doing particularly well with one idea (and then being unable to come up with another one) and in general, trying to re-live glories of the past which are now well past their sell by date.

We can create EFT set ups for these global business and work blockages by asking:

- What were your worst ever work and business related moments?
- What were your best ever work and business related moments?

Make a list and tap through it, one event at a time, to free yourself from the past and gain more energy for the next step into the future.

Business, Work & Relationships

Probably the most important aspect to any type of work and business success is the ability to work well with other people, to understand people, and to build good business relationships.

This also includes people skills, leadership skills, "being a team player if necessary" skills as well and at the same time; and a big hidden X-factor in business and work relationships is whether people actually like you and trust you, or not.

In any type of work situation we will find ourselves in the position where "hard decisions" have to be taken; Mother Theresa was no push over and even though she understood love perfectly well, she also had to be extremely tough to get done what she needed to get done.

Depending on the business you're in, there are certain qualities, skills and relationship aspects that play a big part and you can improve upon any of those with EFT.

You can use the SUE scale to rate "where you are at" and then improve your rating with EFT. This is extremely empowering and has the quite wonderful side effect that we can be powerful AND loving at the same time, thus ending the age old conflict as to how to be a strong leader and a kind leader at the same time.

Here are some ideas to find set ups to improve your work and business relationships.

How would you rate yourself:

- As a leader
- As a team player
- As a colleague
- As a sales person
- As an administrator
- As manager of people
- As a peer to others who do what you do
- As a networker
- As a contributor

- As a speaker/presenter
- As a people person?

You can find more specific roles that are important in your own work and business affairs; and don't just focus on your weak areas. Improving what you are already good at even further can give everything a major boost.

Business & Work Beliefs

Limiting beliefs are always a problem and it is always interesting to test any belief with EFT.

If it is the truth, you can't tap it away but if it is just a limiting belief, interesting things happen when we move this.

In direct response marketing there exists the idea that a 1.5% return from a mailing list is a good response. This is an excellent example of challenging a belief with EFT, and finding out what happens when we do. Within the very first round of EFT, a business person started to laugh and said, "That's a ridiculous number. Where did this come from? Surely it depends entirely on the quality of the mailing list, the offer, how it is all presented. Get it right and why not shoot for a 50% response or even higher?"

Limiting beliefs can hide out in the form of teachings, in proverbs, in daily talk, and particularly in sentences starting out with the words, "Everybody knows that ... (you can't sell a fridge to an Eskimo - oh really ...?)."

Taking some time in business and work to explore the perceived limits and limitations that seem to be set in stone and testing them with EFT can open the way for quite literally floods of new ideas, additional energy, enthusiasm, inspiration and in the end, success.

EFT & Carers

A carer is a person who looks after someone and takes care of them. Today, that term is used for people who take care of relatives in the home; but the concept of being a carer extends further. All parents are carers, even if their children are not disabled or ill; and children become carers to their parents, even if they don't live in or care full time.

Also, there are times when any of us briefly become carers and the challenges then apply to us the same.

In order to care for someone else, first of all a huge amount of energy is required. A carer needs to have full possession of their faculties of mind, body and spirit to perform a wide variety of material, mental and energetic tasks through the day, sometimes through the night as well, and then again, the next day, and the day after that.

This can be a thoroughly overwhelming situation, especially if it is likely to last for a long time and there can be no hope of improvement in the future; and on the material level alone, there is not much that can be done.

When we work with EFT, we work with the energy system, and on that level, we have a lot of power, a lot of potential, a lot of hope and a great deal of leverage to change many things.

The aim as always is to improve the flow of energy through the energy body to make it strong and healthy; to remove blockages and turn stress into positive energy flow as much and as often as we can.

The first order of the day for every carer is to relieve stress.

Please do not underestimate this; carers have a huge accumulation of stress of all kinds, and for a long time.

The added responsibility of taking care of another human being so directly alone can be a huge energetic burden that depresses the entire energy system; plus there are many powerful events along the way which have never been addressed and these drag the energy system down even further. Add to that the huge daily challenges on every level, and it really is no wonder that carers are amongst the most stressed people in society today.

Different people have different ways of describing their stress; whatever the way you think of it and you experience it yourself makes the right set ups for EFT treatments.

We want to release stress by any other name, so we can tap for:

Releasing ...

- Burdens
- Tiredness
- Exhaustion
- Overwhelm
- Desperation
- Misery

This gives us a first relief and a breathing space (literally) and is the first step to improving energy flow.

To further stabilise and nourish the energy system, we then go on to bring in new positive energies and improve the energy flow by tapping on the kinds of energy that will help.

Again, this is individual; choose your own words to describe the kinds of energy you personally need.

We want to draw in

More ...

- Energy
- Love
- Power
- Strength
- Health

This is the baseline pattern for keeping the energy system stable in the face of great daily challenges. It is the foundation for everything else, so it is highly recommended to do this form of EFT treatment at least three times a day, upon rising, during the day, and last thing before going to sleep at night. We also want to apply the stress release → good energy flow at any time it is really needed.

You can think of the energy system as a great waterwheel that has become stuck or is even going backwards; and when we tap EFT, we encourage it to go the other way so it can provide power for the body, mind and spirit alike once again. The more often we can get it to turn the right way, the more it becomes used to it and it will become much harder to knock it backwards again.

When the energy system works properly and energy flows powerfully, the three worst enemies of any carer, mental, physical and emotional exhaustion also begin to recede.

The extra energy that is needed from the carer and which comes from the energy system when it "runs right" then changes quite literally everything - the entire experience of caring becomes different.

Once we have some energy flow, we are also then in a much better position to work with particular challenges and specific problems.

The Caring Relationship

The relationship between the carer and the person who is being cared for is of course central to the experience both will have.

It is a very intense relationship; perhaps the most personal and intimate relationship there is and it therefore produces very intense emotions.

When carers get stressed and overwrought, of course they will exhibit emotions of anger and frustration; many will then feel guilty about feeling that way on top, and all of that further de-stabilises the energy system and makes everything so much harder as a direct result.

In the past, there was literally nothing that could be done to "stop feeling anger" at someone who can't help being what they are and doing what they do; with EFT and energy work, we are in a different place and we can simply address the energy blockages and turn frustration into compassion, anger into love and helplessness into proactive, positive action.

Carers need to really understand that they're not a "bad person" for feeling the way they do on occasion but that they are simply reacting to the stress of their situation in a normal and predictable way.

This is very important so a person can make simple, honest set ups to release the blockages that cause the negative emotions and turn the negatives into positives.

For example, a lady who was caring for her elderly mother felt terribly guilty for having thought on numerous occasions, "I wish she'd die!"

She treated this with EFT, using her own words for the set up, and as the energy started to flow, she realised that she never wanted her mother to die but just wanted to be free to live her own life. Interestingly, after a few more rounds of EFT, when the set up had evolved to, "I love my mother with all my heart," a +10 on the SUE scale, she started to think about hiring someone to sit with her mother for a while, so she could do some of the things that had previously brought her much pleasure (much energy!). She said, "I am absolutely amazed that I never thought of that before. How could I have not realised that? It's so obvious!"

This is what high stress does to a person. The world collapses to the problem, it becomes all there is and we simply don't have the strength in mind, body or spirit to fight our way out of the problem and towards a solution instead.

EFT can be used extremely successfully to deal with all manner of disturbances in the caring relationship. It is extraordinary how tapping on topics that had such a high negative emotional charge before "changes everything."

A gentleman who was looking after his autistic son "just could not stand it when Ben was rolling around on the floor like a lunatic." He would get extremely angry and couldn't control himself any longer in the end, ending up hitting and shaking the boy on one occasion which left him feeling absolutely distraught, guilt riddled and terrified he might hurt Ben badly in the future.

Tapping on the feelings he had with EFT Body Protocol brought up a memory of the first diagnosis when he was told that Ben had autism and he would never be normal. There was a huge amount of energy built up behind that blockage; once it started to flow, Ben's father described the EFT session as "a life changing event, a life saving event, it saved my relationship with Ben, and my own sanity."

Instead of "putting up" with aspects of the caring relationship, when we tap on it with EFT, we can not just solve the problem but transform it to a whole new level.

Ben's father said that the release of the "lunatic" blockage, his relationship with his autistic son had changed completely. He "got more out of" interacting with Ben now, loving him far more unconditionally, finding him fascinating and learning how to relate to him in a different way.

What Ben's father "got more" was additional energy. Ben, autistic or not, has a lot of energy to give from his end. This may not be the kind of energy found in "normal" boys of his age, but it is energy, and as such, it is nourishing - if it can be received by his father.

Taking out blocks and shields that preclude the free flow of energy is the most amazing and truly wonderful experience.

- **We can ask, "What is getting in the way of this relationship?" and simply tap on the answer to that question.**

It is important to do this not just once; but on a regular and ongoing basis to keep the relationship clutter free. Things happen, stress builds up, and this is a process of life. For every relationship, but especially long term caring relationships, we need to ask this question often, to keep the relationship open and energy exchanges flowing freely and clearly.

Proxy EFT In The Caring Relationship

Before EFT, Ben's father may have thought that there is nothing he can do about Ben's problems, his tantrums, his autism, and felt very helpless and desperate because of that.

The dual effects of proxy tapping EFT are a real game changer.

The first effect of Ben's father proxy tapping for Ben is that his own stress, desperation and feelings of helplessness begin to recede, and then turn into positive, proactive feelings, thoughts and behaviours. One of the first things Ben's father said, after having proxy tapped Ben for "his terrible tantrums," was, "I'm not helpless. There are many things I can do. Have done, as well. Will do differently in future!"

The second effect of EFT Proxy Tapping is the mysterious response of Ben's energy system, and therefore, Ben's feelings and behaviours.

Please note that we are not saying we can cure Ben's autism with EFT. Indeed, how much change can be expected in any person's behaviour through proxy tapping cannot be predicted. But we certainly have a new leverage here that did not exist before; a new factor entering into the old problem systems.

This is so for every caring relationship, including and up to sitting by the bed of a dying loved one in the very last moments of their life.

Proxy tapping for the loved ones is an extraordinary experience; it takes the concept of "caring" to a whole new level and the effect on both carer and their charge are truly remarkable.

Transforming The Experience Of Caring

Opening up the caring concept to include real energy exchanges between carer and their charge really does transform the experience of caring.

As one lady explains, "Before EFT, I was trapped in a living nightmare that was so bad I can't even find words for it. I was imprisoned and every day and every night was never ending torture. Then I found EFT and everything changed. It wasn't overnight, and I can't explain it, it was as though I was set free to really help my husband through the last months of his life, to actually be able to give him the love I wanted to give him but I didn't know how. I will be grateful for the rest of my life to EFT."

EFT & Children

It is hard to imagine what kind of people we would be today if those who had cared for us when we were children knew how to do EFT.

What would they have been tapping for ...?

What would they have proxy tapped us for ...?

And would they have taught us how to do EFT so we could help ourselves from a very young age ...?

How would that have changed the course of our lives ...?

It's quite inconceivable really; but we can fairly say that a great many problems and challenges we are facing now need never have come to pass.

EFT & The Child Within

On the bright side, we can certainly proxy tap for our "inner children," the past aspects who are still with us today, and reach out through time and space to them, bring them love and healing, acceptance, forgiveness and reconnection now.

We all have infinite inner children, as all the memories and states of each one is still a part of our energy system today. And amongst those many inner children, there are some which are still in pain, still waiting for something to happen that never did, still waiting for someone to come to their rescue.

We can be that person today; and by proxy tapping for our inner child aspects we can give ourselves a real gift of healing and evolution.

By all means, make a list of inner children of your own. Give each one a specific name such as, "the little boy who was so afraid that mummy would die," or "the little girl who is still waiting for daddy to come back."

With "you" remaining adult, powerful, and firmly in the now, proxy tap for these aspects until you can really feel a lifting, an energizing, a healing across time taking place. Often when we do this, we get a sense of the child smiling at us or waving at us across time as the Healing Event takes place and that feels wonderful.

This is one of the simplest, most direct and powerful ways to resolve old energetic injuries and energy blockages that stem from childhood and it is highly recommended. It really does improve personal power in the now and will also change your self esteem as more and more of "yourself" becomes aligned and there is more energy flow through the entire system.

Also consider that "the child within" may not always be a baby, or a young child; the magic teenager within also needs attention, as does the magic adolescent and the magic person you were yesterday. All our aspects together make up who we are today, and the more energized and happy they are, the happier and more powerful "we, today" become.

EFT & Parents

A lot of problems in children simply stem from the fact that their parents or caretakers are highly stressed. This creates a "stressed world" for the child, causes the child to become stressed, and then we will have two or more very stressed individuals entering into an ever deepening stress loop which can only lead to catastrophe.

If we want to use EFT to "make a better child," then we have to start with the child's world and that is primarily the parents or caretakers.

Parents worry endlessly about their children. On the one hand, that's nice because it shows they care; on the other hand, it makes for a stressful atmosphere where mistakes are going to be made, relationships suffer badly and children become more stressed (and thereby far more stroppy!) in return.

The first order of the day is for the parent to de-stress, and we can start with what they worry about most first of all.

If there are things in the parent's world which stress them so much they forget about the children, we need to tap on those as a first priority.

These days, many families are stressed out of their minds with money worries, with health worries, personal worries. To create a better parent, this stress must be addressed as soon as possible.

Then, we can make a list of what worries us about our children (or grandchildren, step children, adopted children, it matters not) and then apply EFT to one topic after the other.

Here is an example. This lady, Brenda, was very worried that her 10 year old daughter wasn't sociable enough, didn't seem to have any friends and wasn't a part of the in crowd at school.

"Being popular is SO important," she said worriedly, "I was not popular at school and I want so much more for my daughter! I wish she'd make more of an effort to play nice, I keep telling her but she just ignores me ..."

After a couple of rounds of EFT simply to de-stress herself, Brenda started proxy tapping her daughter Shannon using the set up, "Shannon is unpopular!" which produced a real pain in her chest when she thought about it.

She tapped, using the reminder phrase of "unpopular" and soon realised that this was about her own experiences at school which had been very painful for the aspect at the time and still hurt Brenda today when she thought about it.

"I realised I feel that pain of being left out, being unpopular, every time I look at Shannon and think about her. I don't want her to feel that pain. I don't want her to live with that pain."

By this time, Brenda was crying and tapped for, "I don't want Shannon to live with that pain," with the reminder phrase of "that pain."

The pain in her chest started to lift and she felt like she could breathe more deeply. It was then it occurred to her that "this was my pain, not Shannon's. Whatever is wrong with her, I can't help her whilst I'm still in pain myself."

So the next round was for "My pain," and this went down from a -9 to a -4 in the first round. Three more rounds on and the feeling in the chest had become one of openness, "like my heart is more open now, I can be more loving and less afraid."

Brenda tapped on, "More loving," to really improve the energy flow and in that round, she felt an enormous amount of love for Shannon and also for her past aspect, who had been too afraid to be friendly to others at school and that's why she'd been so unpopular.

Brenda said, "I understood so clearly what the problem had been, right back to my mother who had had the same problem, she was always worrying, scared stiff actually, of what the neighbours were thinking and saying and scurried around like a scared mouse all of her life.

"I felt so much love for Shannon who is such a strong person, she'll find her own way. She will do so much better if I stop driving her crazy with my own problems and give her some space to find out who she is and what she wants to do.

"I'll definitely show her how to do EFT and tell her about that fear that ruins everything, I know that now, and I don't have to worry about whether she is popular or not. What I will worry about from now on is whether either of us is afraid of something, and then we can tap on that instead of fighting with each other!"

EFT can really help parents, grandparents and caretakers unblock the free flow of energy in their relationships. It can be used to treat anything that gets in the way of a loving, supporting relationship, be it particular worries, personal hang ups, areas where there are "clashes of will" with the child, dealing with negative emotions "good parents aren't supposed to have" but they all do anyway and then feel guilty about it on top, such as being annoyed by the child, losing one's temper, feeling that one isn't a good parent or that one isn't doing enough and so on and so forth.

As many tens of thousands of parents all over the world can testify, EFT really helps improve relationships across the board and makes for a better parent, grandparent or caretaker - which is certainly something every child deserves.

Tapping EFT With Children

Children have an energy body too and they are very direct in their responses to energy treatments, far more so than the adults who had so much longer to get confused and disassociated from their own feelings.

For young babies, always start with proxy tapping as this is the safest way to do EFT with young and fragile energy systems. Practising the Loving Touch Protocol with very young children and babies is a fabulous experience as well.

You can tap physically on babies, but you need to be very careful. Adults have a powerful energy system and most people don't realise just how much power they have in their healing hands and streaming out of their fingertips. You can very easily upset and "electrocute" a baby or a child by putting through too much power into these sensitive points.

A good way to reign in your healing energy output is to touch the child or baby very gently, like you would stroke the head of a tiny bird with a paper fragile skull to make it feel safe and calm it down. Try this now, using your index finger to very gently touch and stroke the back of your other hand to get a sense of what that feels like.

The same applies for using EFT with young children; be very gentle and use either very soft taps, or gently massage or touch the points instead.

When a child is old enough to learn EFT for themselves and follow you as you demonstrate a treatment round, it is good practice to do some EFT without there having to be a problem first.

Simply show the Heart Healing posture and the points and say together with the child, "Tap, tap, tap!" on each point as a fun activity; you can do this with children as young as 18 months old and it is a lovely energy experience for both of you.

With young children especially, focusing on something good to tap on instead of the more adult way of tapping for a problem is a good way to go.

We can ask a child what it would like, what would make it happy, and tap for that to reduce stress, interrupt unwanted behaviours or calm the child down. For example, 3 year old Bethany who had "a rumble in my tummy" said that she wanted her tummy to feel warm instead. Tapping on "warm tummy" relaxed her, she started to smile and rub her stomach, saying it was warming up and feeling happier. The next round was for "happy tummy" and the pain went away completely; Bethany fell asleep happily only a few minutes later.

In this context, the EFT Body Protocol is particularly useful in all EFT treatments with children, but also teenagers.

Children don't understand the convolutions of naming emotions, and teenagers are very resistant and unwilling to talk about their emotions. By focusing on what they feel in their bodies right now, we stay very reality based and can ask the child for feedback as the sensations start to change.

If you remember that EFT is simply about unblocking the flow of energy and not some kind of psychoanalysis, doing EFT with children is really simple and leads to wonderful changes and evolutions.

EFT & Teenagers

Nowadays, young children turn into "teenagers" at a younger and younger age; and when this happens, a great change also takes place in the family that has to be dealt with correctly.

Once again, this starts with the parents/caretakers who might be confounded by sudden changes in behaviour, emotion and energy of the developing young person.

Many parents suffer actual bereavement when the happy child that once was and with whom they had such a wonderful free flowing relationship turns into a stroppy teenager who seems like a stranger or an alien all of a sudden.

Tapping EFT for this bereavement unlocks the parent's systems and allows them to "let go" of the child-that-was - and in so doing, opens the way for a whole new relationship with the teenager-who-is-here-right-now.

By not clinging on to childish things or trying to return the teenager back into that happy romantic child state, the central reason for a lot of conflict simply disappears and the "stroppy teenager" becomes much less stroppy, literally over night.

EFT can also help parents and caretakers deal with the switches and shifts that happen in a teenager so quickly and seemingly out of the blue; to be more fluent in their dealings with these volatile young people, to learn to understand them better and be able to support them in different ways.

All this should be done first by the parent or caretaker, and *before* we insist that the teenager should learn EFT "to sort themselves out and stop being such a pain in the ass!"

Offered from that position, any teenager worth their salt will be extremely rejecting of EFT, will refuse to try it, and if forced, will sabotage its effectiveness.

Indeed, the most effective way of getting teenagers to see the sense in knowing and doing EFT is for the parent/caretaker to role model how to use EFT for them - to use it on themselves to make themselves a better parent FIRST.

We can then offer the benefits of EFT from a clear and powerful personal standpoint, which is something all people respect, including teenagers.

A good way to introduce EFT for self help to teenagers is to talk simply about stress. Teenagers know all about stress; they have so many things to be stressed about, and a method to deal with that when they are on their own, if honestly offered, will be acceptable to them.

Teaching EFT in the context of stress relief and simply tapping together with the teenager for "stress" improves rapport, and it is the transmission of an important life skill, so it really is worth doing.

This brings us to one more very important point about tapping EFT with children.

Tapping Together

When it comes to energy work and children, we can get stuck in that old idea of needing to fix what is wrong, and that's all there is.

EFT can do much more than that.

Children and young people have very bright energy systems; they are very powerful energy transmitters. They can practically help us with problems of our own, with goals and plans, with making the day brighter if we let them.

"What shall we tap for today?" is the beginning of an energy game that can truly transform the relationship between a child and adult, make it deeper, more joyful, less shielded and less hierarchical.

We can tap together for "happiness," or "sunshine" on a rainy day. For boredom, and as the child grows older, for things that impact the whole family, such as wealth and money, the health of a pet, or even the state of the rain forests if that is a shared concern.

Asking a child to tap with you when you feel low is an amazing thing and really builds self esteem in children - they realise that they have something to give, that their contribution is valuable, and that makes a big difference to many children and youngsters on every level.

Indeed, a whole family can tap together for their hopes and dreams, or to give energy to a plan, dealing with a life change, or just for that feeling of all being together, being in sync, sharing an experience.

This is a truly wonderful and unique thing; and if you would like to experience it yourself but don't think it's possible, make a list of reasons why it couldn't be done and tap on all of them :-)

EFT in families and very much including the children really does have the power to transform relationships beyond the role models we were used to and we grew up with - and that's a wonderful thought indeed.

EFT & Confidence

When there is a good, powerful flow of energy through the energy body, we naturally have confidence in ourselves. This is a kind of confidence which includes a good and rational understanding of the limits of what we can do with mind, body and spirit; and this is important. Many people are rightfully afraid of becoming "over confident" and deluding themselves that they can safely do something when this is not the case. With EFT, we simply take out the blocks to our natural intelligence and our natural abilities to do things as well as we can. This is safe, free of delusions of grandeur, and results in a natural confidence that is very attractive to others too.

In general, people who say they have a problem with confidence, lack confidence or need more confidence, are thinking of a particular set of circumstances where they become stressed, unsure, unbalanced and that leads to a bad performance of some kind.

We can therefore start by asking, "When and where does it happen that you get that feeling of losing your confidence?"

We can then use the EFT Story Protocol to tap through an example.

Terry, a school teacher, felt very confident in her teaching abilities, dealing with students and parents, and in general was a confident and happy person - apart from when she was in meetings with the headmaster or other administrators. Then she felt "as though all my confidence is slipping away from me, I feel like a child myself, tongue tied, blushing, and I can't get my point across."

She wrote out a short story of the last time this had happened to her, starting with, "The headmaster sent me a note that he wanted to see me ..." which caused her to feel nauseous immediately. Terry tapped all the way through the story and at the end was much calmer, and also had realised this had come from her own experiences at school, where she had been terrified of the headmistress. There had been one occasion where she was accused of something she didn't do but she was too stressed out to defend herself. She wrote out the story of that memory and tapped on it too, step by step all the way and then "it was as though this huge, huge cloud lifted away and I could breathe again, and talk again, and I know I can speak up now and get my point across!"

Keith had his confidence crisis when it came to speaking to women; and the more he liked them, the worse it got. He was particularly conscious of the body sensations, starting with a trembling in the arms and hands when thinking about speaking to a lady, which would get worse and cause him physical stomach ache and breathing difficulties. Keith tapped using the EFT Body Protocol, starting with the "trembling hands." After the first round, the trembling was markedly reduced when he thought about speaking to a co-worker and this highlighted the churning in his stomach. This became the next set up phrase. In the EFT round, he burped repeatedly and reported that his stomach seemed to relax and become warm. Next he wanted to tap on his breathing and this resulted in feeling very relieved and clear. He looked forward to speaking to the co-worker the next day.

When it came to it, there was a light trembling in his hands. He went to the toilet and tapped on it, and then went and spoke to the co-worker without fear, but instead with a "curious sense of mild excitement."

A final example on how removing blockages to improve the energy flow helps with natural, healthy confidence comes from Preena. She was taking a course to further her career but after the first training unit lost her confidence in her ability to pass the course. She went back through the training materials to find the places where she had become confused and stressed, and tapped whilst reading those segments out aloud. She reported that "all of a sudden, it was like the lights went on - I'd gotten stuck on the idea that I should know all this stuff, when it was about learning really, my ability to learn! It's ok to not know this, that's what the course is for, to teach me what I don't know! It might sound funny to anyone else but for me that was such a breakthrough. I'm confident that I can learn now, and I want to learn all I can!"

EFT & Depression

Depression from the energetic standpoint denotes a state of the energy system where energy flow has become very low. In extreme cases, we could be dealing with an actual shut down process of the energy system which is structurally similar to what happens during the dying process.

The dying process is a collapse of the energy system from out the outside in; we can think of it as decreasing circles as what little energy there is left is pulled in to shore up the most vital functions at the centre of the energy system. As a hospice nurse described it, "It's like people are in a bubble that gets smaller and smaller. They lose interest in the world, then what goes on in the country, then what goes on with their favourite football club and so on until there's only family left. Then it gets smaller still and it's only them right at the end."

This bubble is the collapsing energy system; and at the centre of the energy system is the heart of energy, the place we put our hands when we do the Heart Healing.

The heart of energy is all important for the functioning of the energy system. When it works well, it empowers all our systems, mind, body and spirit and we feel strong, rejuvenated, alive, bright and happy. When the heart comes on line, like when we are in love, we feel as though we walk on water; and when we consider the the heart of energy as an existing reality, we can also understand how someone can die of a broken heart.

In cases of extreme depression, we want to give the heart as much energy as possible; so we can begin simply by stabilising the heart of energy with the Heart Healing position. This is also helpful as often, very depressed people are simply too depressed to tap; they feel they don't have the energy and can't think of suitable set ups and reminder phrases.

By simply assuming the Heart Healing position and directing what energy the person has to give towards the heart of energy, we can start a stabilisation process and an initial re-energizing at least enough so the person can start to think about tapping and improving their energy flow further.

Depression & Heart Break

There is absolutely a linkage between real depression and the experience of heart break. This would be an event in the person's life that happened before the onset of the depression and in general, people are well aware of what it was that caused their heart to break. This is not a metaphorical description; it is a real description of something that really happened. Matters of the heart, experiences that touch the heart directly, can absolutely cause damage and blockages in the energy system we call the heart centre and when that doesn't function properly, we have every right to say that it is broken.

Luckily, the heart of energy doesn't break like a bone would shatter; it is an energy system and it can be healed with energy. The obvious healing energy for the heart is love by any other name; so to find what love we have and direct it towards the heart is a logical and highly effective way of starting to reverse the processes of depression.

Please note: If your heart was broken, and you find it too painful to think towards the reasons and times when that happened, please engage a professional EFT practitioner to guide you, support you and keep you safe. Nobody would expect from you to do your own open heart surgery; likewise, nobody who is energy aware would expect you to deal with heart break all by yourself.

Self help for depression and broken hearts can certainly get you started and plays a big part in the healing process, but it is important to understand that there is no shame in seeking help for severe structural energy problems. It is simply the right thing to do.

To start the healing process for real depression and a broken heart, we focus on the heart of energy and use Heart Healing at least three times a day but preferably as often as required.

We can then move on to tap EFT on more specific body sensations, using the EFT Body Protocol. We choose this in preference because the feelings in the body are real and we can hold our focus easily on those feelings. We also don't have to worry about finding the right words. With the highest end emotions, there are no words to describe them. "Sadness" isn't sad enough to describe the emotions of heart break; but the pains we feel in our chest are true and right, and they make the best set up statements.

As in all EFT energy work, we want to get flow and movement into the system; we want to improve the energy flow, especially to those areas which are painful for the lack of energy and where obviously the worst blockages and injuries reside.

When we address those core blockages, and a little energy flow starts up, thoughts, emotions and memories emerge naturally. These we can then take and treat with EFT specifically.

At any time you become overwhelmed during the process, return to the Heart Healing to stabilise the energy system. Simple set ups such as "Love," or "Healing" can be used to improve energy flow again.

Depression & Energy Awareness

In all emotional problems, gaining more energy awareness is a high priority to be able to understand how these things happen, how untreated emotions escalate as the warning bells ring louder and louder, and how to intervene at an early stage, and as soon as we notice energy flow is becoming low.

In the long term treatment of depression, energy awareness is absolutely critical.

A person must become very aware of when and how it happens that energy levels drop all of a sudden; how that feels; and what thoughts and emotions follow from those energy shifts, as surely as night follows day.

Depressive and depressing thoughts, such as, "Nobody loves me," "There's no point in even trying ..." "Everything is bad and it can't ever get any better" are only the symptoms of a depleted energy system. They are not the truth; just a part of the warning signs designed to alert us that we need to do something, and do it quickly.

Energy nutrition plays a big part in the long term treatment of depression. A person needs to be aware of what kinds of things are beneficial and nutritious to their energy system, and which will make the energy situation even worse.

For example, many depressed people will gravitate to depressing TV shows and depressing music because there is a resonance match between their energy state and the person who created that depressing content.

Then the depressing energy states enter into a feedback loop with a strong downward spiral, where emotions likewise become more and more distressing and acute as energy levels get lower and lower, and the alarm system gets louder and louder.

With energy awareness, a person can notice when this resonance slide happens and do the Heart Healing instead to raise energy states. This can put them in the position of having enough energy to start thinking about ways to improve energy flow even further.

This can take the form of more EFT, or simply getting up for a moment and breathing fresh air from a window, drinking a glass of water or focusing on something enriching, such as a pet, a house plant or a cloud in the sky.

Understanding what energy is, how it works and what it does to the way we think, feel, act and behave, and the choices we make is of the essence in the long term reversal from depression to leading a purposeful and enjoyable life.

EFT & Dreams

EFT can be used very successfully to unlock the message in a dream so that we can consciously understand what it is about and then hopefully go on to solve the problem that is being presented by the energy mind in this way.

When we talk about EFT and dreams, the first thing everyone thinks about is nightmares, of course. The following simple protocol can be used with anyone who has a bad dream or recurring nightmares as long as they can talk about it afterwards. This includes children as young as three years old. For children who are younger than that and appear to have bad dreams, we recommend you proxy tap for the child instead.

EFT & Nightmares

The first thing to do after a nightmare is simply to de-stress, breathe deeply and do as many treatment rounds of EFT as it takes to really calm down and feel the fear and stress drain away, to be replaced by a feeling of clarity and buoyancy instead.

When energy flow improves, we often remember more details about the dream or begin to understand what it was about, what triggered it; this is natural and of course, very helpful.

Nightmares can be truly terrifying, so to de-stress the energy body is always the first measure, for adults and children alike and also in proxy tapping for younger children or others who cannot tap for themselves.

In many cases, we can learn more about the causes of the nightmare by tapping on the story of the nightmare to move it on to a conclusion.

For example, a young lady dreamed of zombies invading the house she had lived in as a very young child; this was a recurring nightmare that would progress much the same each time. She would find herself a child, in bed, and there would be scratching at the window which frightened her terribly. Then the windows would shatter and the zombies would come in. She would run through the house to try and get out but at every entrance and all the windows, more and more zombies would come in until she would wake up screaming, drenched in sweat, her heart thundering to the point where she was afraid she was going to have a heart attack.

The young lady tapped on what was happening in the story, exactly as though it was a real life situation (*see also EFT & Metaphor*), starting with the scratching at the window. After this round she remembered that there had been a branch outside her bedroom window as a child which, in high winds, would scratch against the glass and terrify her. She was afraid the glass would break. In the dream, the glass breaks and the zombies start clawing through the window. She tapped on that, using "The glass shatters," as set up and reminder phrase. It was then she realised what the dream was all about. Her mother had been pregnant at the time and she had overheard someone saying that her mother could die giving birth; just previously to that, she had seen zombies on the television, dead people. And the dream had come back now because she had just been told that she was pregnant.

Now that she knew what the dream was about, she could tap EFT for her own fears of dying whilst giving birth, and she also proxy tapped her past aspect for being terrified of her mother dying giving birth.

She reports that there was a moment when the fear just went, "like I was a balloon about to pop and then someone let go and the air could just come out and leave me able to breathe again at last. I don't think I've been breathing since that night when I was a child."

Dreams, nightmares and especially recurring nightmares are an attempt from the energy mind to draw our conscious attention to something in the energy system that needs attention, urgently. When we pay attention to such dreams, we are guided to the right places; and with EFT, we can put things to right in a simple and profound way that would be nearly impossible to discover or treat with any other method.

EFT & Dying

Dying is the greatest challenge any human being will ever face; more so if they have time to think about it.

The emotions in the dying process are like no other; they are profound and we have no previous experience to fall back upon when they come to us. Grieving for another is a very different thing and so we go into this endgame without preparation.

There is one thing however that really does change the experience of the dying process, and here I am speaking from personal experience.

- **All the emotions relating to one's own death are still only emotions - movements of energy through the energy body.**

As such, they can be treated with EFT and the emotions will change.

At the same time as our feelings change, our thoughts change too and we think, feel, live differently.

As with bereavement, the first thing to treat if someone is entering into this endgame is the shock of either being told or realising (because it was felt inside) that an end to life is now at hand.

In the past, people reacting to this with "denial" was misunderstood; we are dealing with an energy trauma, an energy blockage or injury that is just the same as any severe trauma in structure, only worse in its effects because it is so very personal.

With this shock blockage in place, energy can no longer flow properly; and there are massive amounts of energy piling up behind that blockage which can cause very severe disturbance. This is clearly something no dying person needs or should have to suffer on top of everything else; so the very first port of call is to de-stress, and then to treat the death shock with EFT as soon as possible.

Please note that it is perfectly ok to experience literally floods of emotions during the treatment of the death shock blockage. This is the pent up energy rushing forth; it's nothing to be afraid of and the person will feel much, much better once the energies started to flow and then settle down again.

Holding the Heart Healing posture keeps a centre for the person and will help them come back to themselves and stabilise. When the death shock blockage has been released, we can go on to treat more specific emotions and other emotions.

These too are immensely powerful but if we can keep the focus on energy movements, by remembering that "this is only energy," that it must flow and when it does, we feel better, we can begin to learn to ride these powerful waves of emotions in a different way.

This is a valuable thing to do and transforms the experience of the last times spent in body and on Earth for a person; this is a very precious time, an important time in a person's life.

EFT In The Dying Process

There comes a time when a person can no longer treat themselves with EFT; and we might be in a position of being the other, the one who is watching and supporting another person's dying process.

Seeing or knowing one's loved ones to be terribly upset is very painful to people who are dying and it adds to their problems, de-stabilises them even further and this becomes ever more problematic, the more fragile the energy system of the dying person becomes.

Conversely, a forced "jolly hockey sticks" stiff upper lip attitude is no help either; to have a person support one's dying process whose energies are flowing smoothly and who is able to focus on giving love and support - energies, these are - without falling apart themselves is the greatest gift one can give to a dying person.

Indeed, the gift of energy exchanges is in the end, the only thing that remains to be given beyond basic care taking; and to be able to do something for yourself, and for the loved one who is dying in and of itself changes the experience of the dying process for both parties absolutely.

It is here, in the highest end of human emotional experiences that the power of modern energy work really makes itself felt and quite literally starts to shine.

Being able to flow emotions successfully transforms the dying experience on every level challenges much that we thought was inevitable and unavoidable, especially the severe emotional suffering that we have come to expect at the end of days.

I would like to leave us with the thought that modern energy work may yet be the proof positive that love really does transcend all, and that all that remains in the end, is love.

EFT & Emotions

The original EFT discovery statement was that "all negative emotions are a disruption in the energy system."

This is true; and as more was learned about the relationship between emotions and the energy body, it was discovered that in fact,

- **"All emotions are the physical sensations resulting from movements of energy through the energy body."**

We have summed this up by saying, "This is only energy!" in the face of all human emotions, from the worst to the best; and this understanding unlocks the mysteries of human emotions, full stop.

Modern energy work takes away the fear of emotion and makes emotions logical and easily understood, easily explained.

Moreover, it makes emotions real.

- **Emotions are physical feelings in the physical body that have no physical origin.**

As such, we can now describe emotions in a different way, using a direct and clean language of actual body sensations. This avoids misunderstandings and makes emotions easy to understand to any human being at all.

When we stop thinking about emotions in terms of labels such as anger, grief, sadness, disappointment, unhappiness and so forth and instead start to describe what we can physically feel in our own bodies, we can begin to communicate about our emotions in a whole new way.

When we say to a young child, "I am very upset," the meaning of this could be anything. When we say to the same child, about the same emotion we are feeling, "My head is hot and hurts!" a three year old child understands that and may even offer to fetch a wet cloth to cool the head down. This is practical emotional support on a whole new level; here we have an opportunity to not just understand what other people are really feeling, but also a straightforward invitation to do something about this, and help them with their emotional problems.

Many men, for example, don't want to talk "about" their emotions in the old fashioned psychoanalysis sense. However, they are perfectly capable of describing the physical effects of certain situations, such as trembling in the hands, churning in the stomach, pressure in the head and so forth which another person might be interpreting as, "I'm upset," or "I'm angry," or "I'm jealous."

This new, precise and accurate language of emotions makes for direct and hard hitting EFT set ups and amazingly fast resolutions to emotional problems that would have kept a person in talking therapy for decades.

We should also not underestimate what it does for a person who feels powerful emotions that drive all manner of seeming crazy or inexplicable behaviours and thoughts when they find out that their problems are real, they are not "all in their minds," that there really is a good reason for having these problems, and that the reason is to be found in the energy system.

To start to understand how the state of our energy system quite literally makes us feel the way we do has the power to transform people's self concept in an instance.

Instead of being irretrievably damaged, crazy or insane, when we re-discover the amazing logic of the causes and effects of our own problems, quite literally, everything changes.

We understand ourselves better.

We understand other people better.

This is a huge stress relief that applies to everything we do and everyone we meet.

At the same time, discovering how one's own energy system creates emotion, and how these emotional states dictate what we think and what we do, allows us to ask whole new questions, think brand new thoughts, and re-think many of the decisions we have made along the way.

For example, when a person discovers that they are not crazy but simply suffering from an assortment of energy blockages that can be removed with EFT, what does that mean for that person's life?

What does that mean for the way they think about themselves, what they want and need, what they can achieve?

Losing the fear of emotions is an extraordinary breakthrough for any human being. It enables a person to consider undertaking tasks that were previously deemed too difficult, too painful and to unachievable. It enables a person to release negative emotions, but also to go into a future where they don't have to be afraid of loving and losing, yet again, for example. Or where they don't have to be afraid of trying and failing.

This truly is a paradigm shift for each individual person who understands the truth about energy and emotions; and globally speaking, a paradigm shift for humanity at large.

It is also important to remember that when we use EFT, we do not just tap negative emotions away. As marvellous as that is, the paradigm shift lies in taking the energy flow further until we start to feel good instead - the bright side of the SUE scale.

Here, a person's real potential becomes finally revealed.

When energy flow hits +8 and above, we wake up to a new reality of being, one where there is not just joy, faith and love, but where we are really are thinking better, feeling better and have much more power to create our own reality than we have ever had before.

People who thought they were stupid find out that they can think beautifully clearly and logically.

People who thought they can't sing find out that they can sing, and sing well, at that; people who thought they were weak find out that in fact, they can be strong.

People who thought they were ugly discover their own beauty; and people who thought they were irretrievably damaged find a healing.

This is amazing, wonderful but most of all, it is true.

"Emotional freedom" is not just a phrase. It is a state of being that we can touch for real when we improve energy flow beyond that hideous Zero Point of Nothing, or hope for "feeling nothing at all" as the best a human can get.

And all of that is simply an example that when we get something right, it works.

Emotions & Problems

When we work with EFT, we can't change reality; we can't change the world. What we do change is our emotions relating to reality, and so what happens is that we change our own world, one person at a time.

As EFT works strictly with the energy system and energy occurrences, we can discover through the medium of our emotions where the problem we have with someone or something really lie.

In the old counselling models, clients were perpetually driven to distraction by the question, "And how do you feel about that?" in response to any given problem a person would bring to the session.

"My business is failing ..." - "And how do you feel about that?"

"My health is failing ..." - "And how do you feel about that?"

"My cat has run away ..." - "And how do you feel about that?"

When we take that question seriously and consider that whatever the energy blockages are which are causing us problems are actually felt in the physical body, and that's what the kinds of feelings the counsellors were asking about really are, we can finally answer that vexed question.

Only, it's not so much, "How do you feel about that?" but rather, "And where do you feel that in your body?"

When you think about your business failing, where do you feel that in your body? Show me with your hands.

That place, wherever it may be, is where the blockage in the energy body exists that cause sensations of heat or cold, of pressure or emptiness, of stuckness, churning, nausea or actual physical pain.

When we direct our EFT round upon that very place, "that churning in my stomach (that I feel when I think about my failing business)" we are treating the real emotion relating to this problem.

We can use that question, "Where do you feel this in your body? Show me with your hands!" to directly locate energy blockages and treat them swiftly and easily.

The feedback we receive from our own physical feelings guides us through the process and gives us information how our "emotions" are changing and evolving, from round to round, from set up to set up.

Expanding The Concept Of Emotions

Now that we know that emotions are physical feelings that tell us (precisely!) about the state of our energy body, and (precisely!) where the disturbances are located, we can understand that emotions are more than just anger, sadness and so forth.

Emotions exist on a wide range from tiny fleeting sensations that are usually entirely unnoticed, via the so called "intuition" or "gut feelings" to what was formally thought of as emotions, the usual anger, sadness etc.

But then emotions go on further into feelings that have no names, and in the end manifest in psychosomatic pain, which has become indistinguishable from acute physical pain.

This is the structural reality of emotions; and this simple observation unlocks a myriad of unanswered questions and previously perplexing reasons for why people do the things they do.

Knowing that all these emotions, across the whole scale, are nothing but status reports from the energy system, and that we can now pay attention, heed their call and do something about it with EFT is an extraordinary breakthrough, the magnitude of which we can't quite conceive of yet.

Ignoring emotions, which is what humans have been taught to do in all known civilisations so far, leads into a cul-de-sac of stress and madness, from which there can be no escape.

The human energy body is transmitting essential information not just about its own state of functioning, but also about energy occurrences in the environment - what is going on with other people's energy systems, with the energy outputs from everything, as everything exists also at the energy level.

Without adding this essential 6th sense information to what we have gleaned from the other five senses, almost all real problems can never be solved at all.

And it is the absence of this additional information that has led humanity into the crazy, illogical and totally confusing systems and ways of doing and being we see all around us today.

By giving modern people a practical way to not just deal with their emotions, but to understand why we have them, why they are so important, and what we can do to "feel differently" modern energy work and EFT are giving us access to an additional data set that is the missing X-factor in humanity's equations across the board.

EFT & Emotional Intelligence

In recent years, the idea of "emotional intelligence" has been posited; that intelligence is not just about being able to crank out equations like a super computer, but that there is a form of natural intelligence that allows a person to "compute" the emotional behaviours of other people.

Without understanding what emotions are and how they work, it was thought that it was very difficult to improve emotional intelligence; with our new emotions = energy movements paradigm, we can all become far more emotionally intelligent.

Emotional intelligence starts at home, with the conscious understanding that emotions are real feelings in the body which every person experiences, but some people have banded together and labelled certain feelings "anger," and others "sadness," "disappointment," "worry," and so on and so forth.

When we drop the labels and instead consider the real physical feelings we experience in response to our changing environments, we start to learn something about the nature of the emotional experience - and the more we learn about how emotions work, the more emotionally intelligent we become.

People have tried forever and a day to "master their emotions." Unfortunately, they went about it the wrong way, by trying to train themselves to ignore the feelings in their body.

This is like trying to master the English language by training oneself to ignore all incidences of language, letters and words in the environment and never to speak, hear or write a single sentence, ever; a truly preposterous undertaking that is doomed to fail before it even starts and can only lead into insanity.

If we want to master our emotions, we first of all have to pay attention to them and take notice of them. We need to gain experience with our own emotions, and that does not just mean life disabling fits of rage, grief and depression, but the whole range of emotions, from the lightest, most fleeting sensation such as a shiver down the back in a warm room when a stranger enters, all the way past every day emotions, and into the psychosomatic emotions. We must also learn to pay attention to our positive emotions again, from the smallest wry little smile all the way out to raucous laughter, tears of joy and heart-bursting gladness and pride as well.

When we start with EFT, we have a way into that "language of emotions" which is a profoundly complex language made up from a thousand and one body sensations, the energy body playing the physical body like not just a single instrument, but a huge orchestra. All of that is information, and all that information is information we really need to make sense of the world and our lives.

By practising the Mindful EFT Protocol and really paying attention to how it feels in the body when we think about something, and touch those special energy points; how each point causes different sensations in different locations; how we can feel pathways as sensations travel around our body, all of this is the basic ABC of understanding our own emotions, first of all.

Combined with the fact that when we have learned EFT, we don't need to be afraid of emotions any longer as people once were, we have a clear and wonderful pathway towards discovering our own "emotional intelligence."

Of course, we will be able to notice how emotions work in other people with practice and experience too.

Unlike the common state of being, where stressed out people stress out other stressed out people even more until the bough breaks, we can recognise our own stress, de-stress ourselves and then react to the other stressed people in a different way.

We can invite them to de-stress also; we can keep ourselves calm and energized, a beacon of light that can help others relax, simply because we're there.

Whatever we do, we can make new decisions and we can evaluate our fellow human beings differently, understand them better and that is when true emotional intelligence begins to emerge.

We have a long way to go as we re-learn to understand our own emotions again which have been ignored for so long; but every round of EFT we tap helps us improve our own emotional intelligence, and in the end cannot help but lead to a form of emotional mastery the likes of which the world has never known before.

EFT & Events

All people have an energy body, but in the Western world we behave as though we don't.

As a result, the energy body is overlooked when it comes to trying to figure out how a problem has come into being.

For example, "everybody knows" that a person who is afraid of big black dogs must have had some kind of an experience involving a big black dog which caused them to become afraid in the first place.

If the person was bitten by the dog, even the scar might already be fading away as the physicality restores itself, so where is that memory located which is causing a person decades after the original event to still become terrified when they see a black dog on TV?

In the past, people thought "it was all in the mind."

We now say that there may be an aspect to that, but the problem is certainly stored as a disruption or blockage in the energy system.

This is why EFT works, and why people experience their emotions changing when we tap on the energy points.

- **For the problems we have today, there is always a corresponding blockage in the energy system.**

- **This blockage was caused by an event of some kind - an energy body event.**

Sometimes, the energy body event happens at the same time as a physical event, for example if someone is shot unexpectedly, or breaks their leg in an accident, or is bitten by a dog. The physical injury is treated and the physical part of the totality gets better, but the energy system receives no such treatment and so remains disturbed and damaged.

The energy system can also be affected by things which don't touch the physicality at all. For example, a person might experience a powerful energy system event when someone says something to them, or even looks at them in a certain way at the right time.

The old saying, "Sticks and stones can hurt my bones but words can never hurt me," is actually incorrect. Words, or rather the energy behind the words, can hurt people very badly and cause life long wounds in the energy system, much longer lasting suffering and worse side effects than a beating with a big stick.

When we talk about energy body events, *moments in time which changed the energy system profoundly in an instance*, it really doesn't matter if such an event was caused by a massive tragedy or a single look at the wrong time.

There was damage done, and we can know this by the symptoms and problems a person developed after the fact.

If there ever was a time before the problem started, there has to have been an event which caused this.

When we work with EFT and events, we clearly cannot cure illness, accident, physical damage. But what we can do is to remove blockages from the energy system relating to those events, and then we feel differently about the events in our lives.

Types Of Events

We have four types of events - energy body events - we can treat with EFT.

Trauma Event

The first is the trauma event. This is when something frightening, painful or disturbing happened, really upset the energy system and unbalanced the entire mind/body/spirit system dramatically.

Many problems - but by no means all problems! - have their root or genesis in a trauma event.

Guiding Star Event

The second type of events are the Guiding Stars. Instead of being particularly painful or frightening, here a person has a particularly good experience in the energy system.

This causes a kind of "falling love" with what was in the environment at the time, and leads to fetishes, addictions, collections, hoarding, and generally obsessively repeating actions over and over again to feel that good feeling again.

Unknowable Event

The third type events are called the Unknowable Events. We can't say whether it was good or bad, just that something did happen, and life was never the same again afterwards.

Missing Event

The fourth type of events are missing events. These are things that should have happened, but they did not; and the energy system tries to recreate those missing events to complete itself and evolve.

Missing events are often at the root of problems that revolve around feeling empty, feeling lost, or having a sense that one is searching for something but it is not known what one is searching for, or where to find it.

 Each event caused the energy system to change significantly in some way; and since the event, the energy system got stuck in that state and this is what is causing the problems today.

When we bring movement and flow back into the energy system, it can evolve beyond that old event and a person is set free to have new experiences instead of repeating old experiences in the form of event echoes over and over again.

Genesis Event & Event Echoes

When the energy system gets stuck due to an event, it will replay that event repeatedly to draw attention to the problem, and it will continue to do so until something is done about it.

The original event, or genesis event, sets up a sequence of echoes.

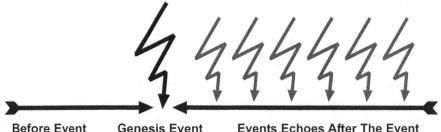

Before Event   Genesis Event   Events Echoes After The Event

These are like repeat performances of the original event; even when the actors, sets and props have changed, the story remains the same.

In trauma events, the echoes can be unwanted flashbacks to the trauma event, intrusive thoughts and emotions relating to the trauma event, and instant flaring up of thoughts and emotions when the memory of the event is triggered. These symptoms are now called collectively "post traumatic stress disorder" or PTSD.

In Guiding Star events, a person is driven to seek out the same thing over and over again - a certain type of person, a certain type of shoe, a certain type of artefact, a certain type of food etc.

As with the trauma flashbacks, a person has no control over this; the conditions in the energy system will represent the stuck state over, and over, and over again until the system is unstuck and can evolve beyond the Guiding Star.

 Any serially repeating behaviour, thought or emotion that is not under the control of their owner tells us there is a genesis event and it is still echoing - here is a problem in the energy system which is seeking our attention and will continue to do so until we address it.

Treating Events With EFT

When we work with EFT and the energy body, we do not need to know the genesis event - the first, causative event - in order to bring back flow and unstick the energy system.

We can work with an echo instead; a recent example of the problem in action.

For example, a person who suffers from panic attacks and doesn't remember when they had their first ever panic attack can use the most recent panic attack and treat that one with EFT.

We can use the story of the panic attack and the EFT Story Protocol to improve energy flow; the echo event is a way into the whole problem group, which consists of the genesis event, and all the echoes ever since.

We can ask, "Tell the story of the last time you had a panic attack."

Important! When we start to think about real events of any kind, we are naturally going to become stressed. We are tuning towards an energy body state that is definitely blocked, disturbed and might have been stuck for a very long time.

 We always need to build a stress free path into the event.

In practice, this means to do as many rounds as it takes so that you don't feel stressed but empowered, ready and willing to engage with that event.

In our example, the person with the panic attacks wanted to start with, "Even thinking about the last time I had a panic attack makes me very scared!" with a reminder phrase of, "Very scared!"

At the end of that round, their "very scared" had gone from a -7 to a -3, and they did another round for, "I'm still very stressed thinking about my panic attack last week," with the reminder phrase of, "Very stressed."

After that round, they felt ready to start telling the story of the last panic attack, which happened last week in a shopping centre car park.

De-stressing and energizing before we get into the problem story is very important and really helpful. In self help, do pay attention to this and make sure you are ready and willing to start thinking about the problem story and that you feel clear and calm

Now we can go into the EFT Story Protocol and tap every sentence fragment if necessary, one after the other, until we can really feel that there is movement in thought, emotion, body and energy.

That way we are building a safe path towards the heart of the problem, the moment when something profound happens in the energy system, which likewise has a profound effect on the person.

Here are the steps of the person with the panic attack in the car park.

Each line represents its own round of EFT as the person goes through the Story Protocol, one line at a time.

Set up 1: I was already worried about panicking before I even left home and took a tranquillizer. Reminder phrase: Tranquilliser.

Set up 2: I felt really wobbly in the car, sick to my stomach. Reminder phrase: Sick to my stomach.

Set up 3: The car park was chock full with cars there was nowhere to park and I was dreading the walk to the entrance. Reminder phrase: walk to the entrance.

Set up 4: When I got out of the car, the distance to the entrance felt like a thousand miles away and it stretched out ever further like everything had become liquid and unstable. Reminder phrase: Liquid and unstable.

Set up 5: That's when I couldn't breathe any more ... Reminder phrase: I could not breathe

Set up 6: ... and my heart was exploding ... Reminder phrase: Heart exploding.

Set up 7: ... and I wanted to scream but I couldn't ... Reminder phrase: Screaming.

Set up 8: ... and I thought I was going to die. Reminder phrase: I was going to die, switching to, I didn't die midway through the round.

The person then remembered when the first time was that they had experienced a panic attack; "I didn't die" was the turning point in the treatment.

They decided to leave the genesis event for another time and finished the session by doing a couple of rounds of EFT for "life energy" which felt perfect to them and made them smile.

Here are the main points once more in brief.

- The energy system becomes disturbed during a real event. This disturbance will produce significant "after" symptoms that were not there before the event and these symptoms will remain and can get worse if the disturbance remains untreated.

- Real events always echo - they will represent themselves over and over again until the disturbance is treated.

- In energy work, we don't need to start with the genesis event. We can start by treating a recent echo instead which is also a good way in.

- We always start with de-stressing rounds before we get into the story of the event. Take as much time and as many rounds as you need to feel comfortable and ready and willing to tell the story of the event.

- Now we can treat the story, step by step, with as many rounds of EFT as it takes until the whole story is done.

- Very importantly, we end the session with a few extra rounds to bring positive energy flow to the energy system so we feel good and empowered at the end.

Please note: It is perfectly possible to treat events with EFT is self help - if you follow through and de-stress and re-energize yourself properly along the way.

For very daunting events and memories, we recommend you work with a qualified EFT practitioner who can help you de-stress, assist you and support your throughout the process and who can add their energy and intelligence to the process to make it as elegant, easy and stress free as possible.

EFT & Forgiveness

All major world religions tell us that we have to forgive those who have hurt us - but they generally don't tell us how we are supposed to do that.

With EFT, forgiveness becomes easy and very logical.

When we sustain an energetic injury, we feel painful emotions; now, we are in pain. The worse this pain is, the more we hate those who have caused us this pain in a direct cause-and-effect connection. We will continue to hate them and have to continue hating them until the pain goes away. When it does, we are ready to forgive them - and not one second earlier.

In order to achieve real, proper forgiveness we need to first of all focus on the pain itself. Often, it is easiest to use the EFT Body Protocol - where do you feel the pain still today? Show me with your hands.

That is the location of the real energetic injury which needs to be healed.

"I want to heal this pain in my heart," with the reminder phrase of, "Pain in my heart," would be an example to get us started.

A note: It is very useful to take a SUE scale reading of how bad the pain is that you are suffering from still. This makes it consciously clear that you really are in pain, it is not all in your head, there really is an injury which needs to be treated.

By focusing on the pain and the real injury, we don't have to worry for now whether it is good or bad to forgive someone, what happened, who did what to whom, where, why or any of those many things that are just an effect of a stressed person who is in real pain.

Once the pain has lessened, please keep tapping to really re-energize that place that had been in pain for so long. Tap additional rounds of EFT for bringing new, fresh energy into that place, for example, "I want my heart to be whole and strong," as a set up with "whole and strong" as a reminder phrase. In a real life example of this process, a lady who had been raped chose the set up of, "My shining heart," towards the latter stages of the treatment to bring the energy flow right up towards the +10 on the SUE scale.

With the pain transformed, we can consider the perpetrator/s or those we need to forgive.

What you will find is that your thinking and feeling has changed dramatically and you are now ready to consider to forgive this person and what that means.

Please note: While we are still in emotional pain, we naturally think and feel that we should not forgive the perpetrator/s because (xxx). Because that would validate their behaviour, reward them, encourage them to do it again, all sorts of thoughts and feelings will naturally go through our minds and bodies.

These thoughts disappear when the pain disappears and are replaced by other thoughts.

The new thoughts are about becoming free of the emotional strands that are still binding us to the perpetrator/s, and that this isn't about them at all, but about our own healing process instead.

When these thoughts and feelings come, then we are ready to take a deep breath and tap, "I forgive X" for the first time - and let the EFT magic take its course.

If you are not ready to tap this set up, please know that it is simply the fact that you are still in pain and the original injuries have not yet been healed completely. You need to treat the injuries further. Ask yourself, "And what else stands between me and real forgiveness?" and in extreme cases we strongly recommend you work with an experienced EFT practitioner by your side.

Real forgiveness is a fantastic experience; it is immeasurably freeing but also energizing, life affirming. It is something that every victim deserves absolutely, without exceptions and thanks to modern energy work, is now achievable at last.

EFT & Freedom Spells

"All of my sadness, I now let you go; soften and flow, soften and flow!"

This is an example of a set up which is borrowed from EmoTrance and which is known as a Freedom Spell.

When we tap this with EFT, we say the whole thing on each one of the points and in the Heart Healing position.

Remember to breathe deeply in and out between points.

Also pay attention to how it feels when things really start to flow away and old blockages, reversals are relieved and the energy stored up behind them gets to flow out at last. This is a very relaxing and healthy exercise, and you can choose anything that you wish to flow away.

Here are some examples; pick one that jumps out at you and have a go to experience this for yourself.

Abilities	*Beauty*	*Cruelties*
Abuse	*Beliefs*	*Crutches*
Abusers	*Betrayals*	*Curses*
Accidents	*Bindings*	*Damage*
Accusations	*Blessings*	*Damnation*
Accusers	*Blocks to my magic*	*Deceit*
Achievements	*Blocks to the future*	*Defeats*
Affectations	*Boredom*	*Definitions*
All that still hurts me	*Borders & Barriers*	*Delights*
All that still scares me	*Bravery*	*Delusions*
All that still limits me	*Brutal criticisms*	*Delusions of Grandeur*
All that still blocks me	*Burdens*	*Demons*
Ambitions	*Clowning*	*Depression/s*
Ancient Entrainments	*Clumsiness*	*Descriptions*
Angers	*Commands*	*Desires*
Answers	*Complaints*	*Despair*
Anxieties	*Conclusions*	*Desperation*
Allegiance/s	*Connections*	*Dilemmas*
Allergies	*Constrictions*	*Dirtiness*
Altruisms	*Contortions*	*Disappointments*
Appraisals	*Contracts*	*Dislikes*
Arrogance	*Controls*	*Dissatisfaction*
Aspirations	*Courage*	*Distress*
Bad habits	*Cowardliness*	*Divisions*
Badness	*Craziness*	*Doubts*
Barriers	*Crimes*	*Dramas*
Barriers to (...)	*Criticisms*	*Dreams*

Duties
Ego/s
Enemies
Enslavements
Entrainments
Envy
Embarrassments
Emptiness
Evil
Excuses
Expectations
Errors
Exhaustions
Failure/s
Fears
Fears and Judgements
Findings
Fights
Flirtations
Flights of Fancy
Fog
Foggy Thinking
Foolishness
Foolhardiness
Freedoms
Friends
Friends & Lovers
Frozen energies
Frustrations
Games
Genetics
Ghosts
Ghosts of the past
Gifts
Goals
Good habits
Goodness
Gratitude
Greed
Gremlins
Grief
Grimness
Guilt
Guilty Feelings
Habits
Happiness
Hatred
Hopes
Hungers
Hurtful (...)
Hurtful Decisions
Ideas
Ideas about (...)
Ideas about people

Ideas about me
Illnesses
Illusions
Imaginings
Injustice
Insanities
Interventions
Irritations
Instances of (...)
Jealousy
Jewels
Joys
Judgements
Kindness
Knowledge
Laws
Laziness
Learnings
Lies
Lies and Deceit
Life Lines
Likes
Limitations
Logic
Logical Fallacies
Loneliness
Longings
Loves
Madness
Malcontent
Maps
Measures
Memories
Memories of injustice
Memories of pain
Mind Games
Misery
Mercy
Merits
Misplaced Allegiances
Misplaced (...)
Mistakes
Mistreatments
Monsters
Monstrosity
Morals
Morals and Values
Naivety
Niceness
Nightmares
Neediness
Negative Feelings
Obligations
Old Wives Tales

Opinions
Oppressions
Oppressors
Orders
Orders & Commands
Paranoia
Parts
Patience
Perturbations
Perversions
Pictures
Pictures of (...)
Pity
Plans
Plans & Goals
Positive Feelings
Possessions
Post Hypnotic Suggestions
Powers
Power Games
Prisons
Problems
Problems with (...)
Promises
Prejudices
Pretensions
Pretend (...)
Prides
Procrastinations
Punishment
Questions
Racial Burdens
Rage
Rat Races
Reality
Real (...)
Responsibilities
Restrictions
Reticence
Revenge
Revenge Fantasies
Reversals
Rewards
Righteous Indignation
Romantic Delusions
Routine/s
Scales
Sensations
Sensible Solutions
Sensitivity
Self Pity
Self Mutilations
Self Love
Self Hatred

Self Destruction	Stupidity	Unreasonable Nonsense
Self Satisfaction	Suffering	Untruths
Self Doubt	Surrenders	Vanity
Separations	Suspicions	Victories
Salvations	Talents	Views
Shields	Tensions	Violence
Shocks	Ties	Voices
Shadows	Ties to (...)	Vows
Shoulds	Tiredness	Walls
Shyness	Tired Old Games	Wants
Snide Comments	Toys	Wars
Silences	Torments	Waterloos
Silliness	Tormentors	Weakness
Sins	Tortures	Weariness
Skills	Torturers	Wild Accusations
Slave Mentality	Traumas	Wisdom
Slavery	Trainings	Wishes
Solutions	Triumphs	Words
Sounds	Trust	Works
Soulful Sighs	Truths	Worries
Stoppers	Ugliness	Wounds
Stored Up Resources	Unfounded (...)	Wrongful Decisions
Stress	Unfounded Accusations	Years
Stressors	Unfulfilled (...)	Yearnings
Superstitions	Unfulfilled Desires	
Stubbornness	Unhelpful Orders	

"Letting go" of things energetically improves energy flow and makes us feel better. Sometimes, even positives such as "beauty" and "intelligence" or special talents can be a burden on a person if they're not flowing right energetically.

After the EFT treatment round with the Freedom Spell of your choice, you can do an energizing round by simply tapping for "energy" or if you like, qualifying this with attributes you find particularly pleasant and exciting, such as, "beautiful energy," "bright energy," "heavenly energy," etc.

Choose something to make you feel spectacularly good, that's what EFT is for!

164

EFT & The Genius Factor

Over the last decade, it has been established that what we need in order to think at the genius level is to take a different point of view to the flow of information between the conscious mind and the energy mind.

Previously known as the sub- or unconscious mind, the energy mind is essentially the head of the energy body and processes information quite differently. It adds a different level of information and works with much more information rich, ever evolving data in real time.

The energy mind is, however, not the genius mind; the genius mind happens when the energy mind and the conscious mind start to co-operate and there is a free flow of information between them.

When the energy mind and the conscious mind get into sync, they become more than the sum of their parts and real "genius" happens.

When that happens, even for a very short period of time, "genius insights" and genius solutions occur. The oft quoted light bulb over the top of the head is a nice representation of a factual event in the energy system when energy flow is increased to the point where "the lights come on," the Eureka event happens, and a true genius solution has been found.

Intelligence, Creativity & Stress

Every human being who walks the Earth today and does not have severe damage in their physical brain has the hardware to think at the genius level.

This is no more mysterious than to say that everyone who has functional eyes can see, and everyone who has functional legs can walk.

How well all and any of that functions is firstly related to stress.

- **The more stressed a person, the more stupid they become in a direct cause and effect relationship.**

This is so because stress de-stabilises everything and that certainly includes the capacity for logical thought at every level.

Apart from de-stabilising the capacity for thought overall, the more stress is present, the more the energy mind is disconnected from conscious awareness.

Writers, artists and other creatives know this well and have much experience with the de-stabilising effects of stress which soon enough lead to "writer's block" - an absence of the flow of creative ideas and insights, a "drying up" of the stream of creative ideas, which are data streams from the energy mind.

So and once again, to establish a baseline of intelligence we need to de-stress and re-energize first of all.

As an exercise in less stress = more intelligence, try this now.

- Think about a big problem you have and that really worries (stresses you). Now, do one round of EFT simply for "Stress."

- Think about the problem again and notice how you are thinking differently when stress recedes.

- Tap another round on stress and notice how your thinking gets clearer, more organised, more logical and more expansive the less stressed you become, and the more energized you start to feel.

- Keep going and bring in more energy, increase the flow to a +10 and allow yourself to be amazed at the solutions to the problem that are available to you all of a sudden.

Gaining Access To The Bigger Picture

If you go on to improve the flow of energy through your entire system until you get onto the positive wing of the SUE scale, you will notice how your thinking becomes smarter, more focused, more wide ranging, more inclusive of information, how the "bigger picture" is beginning to emerge.

Of course, this is not just a picture; it's the "bigger information" as our mind/body/spirit systems are starting to find a better level of functioning together.

Improve your energy flow until it is at +10 and you really can expect a genius solution to your big problem to flash into your mind.

Is it that simple?

Yes, it is.

It is structural for genius type thinking to kick into action as the energy flow through our energy bodies begins to improve to the point that the energy mind re-engages with all the rest of our systems, and the conscious mind is stress free enough to actually NOTICE what the energy mind is sending us.

So our next step beyond simple stress relief in order to access genius solutions and genius answers is to use EFT to improve energy flow relating to the topic you are investigating to a +10.

That really is the EFT Genius pattern in a nutshell. You can apply this to all and every problem and it will work, providing you stay on track and you keep going until you have achieved a +10 in energy flow on that topic.

Creativity & The Energy Mind

The process of creativity relies on streams of information from the energy mind which are received consciously and then acted upon.

For all creative solutions, we need the energy mind to "send us" information in the form of visions - not just pictures, but a full body experience like you would have in a dream and which includes information about sight, sound, feel, taste, scent and most importantly, information from the 6th Sense, how all of that makes us feel inside through the medium of emotions.

It has been discovered that the energy mind is sending this creative information all the time, we are just too stressed to notice.

Energy Blocks To Genius Information

Contrary to public opinion, one genius idea in a whole lifetime is not enough to call yourself a real genius.

Being a genius is to be able to access the data streams from the energy mind at will and all the time, and thus bring "genius thinking" to bear on all aspects of your life.

This is how we were designed to work; conscious mind and energy mind working together in harmony and essentially producing a single, smoothly flowing system that is more than the sum of its parts.

- **Every person alive today has significant blocks in their energy system which preclude free flow of information from the energy mind to the conscious mind and vice versa.**

What these blocks are can be highly individual and can come about from all manner of previous experiences, from traumatic experiences with learning, bad experiences with energy mind generated materials such as dreams and visions, hearing voices and such, to Guiding Star experiences with having a single good idea and "getting stuck" on that one idea, which also precludes more new good ideas flowing freely and all the time.

We can simply ask the question,

"What stands in the way of my genius today?"

... and provided we're not so stressed that we generate a lot of meaningless stress talk, we will be able to make a list of our own personal "genius blockages."

If you are not ready to consider yourself a genius, you can start somewhere else.

For example, you can rate yourself on the SUE scale as to how naturally creative you are and simply tap that up until you hit the +10.

Or you could rate your intelligence, capacity for logic, or any other type of mind function and apply EFT until you have it at a +10.

Or you might feel you're a +10 for intelligence, but not quite there for "emotional intelligence" and this could do with some improvement. Here, too, get the SUE scale out and start tapping to do nothing other than improve the flow of energy through your energy body until you start to feel, think and experience very differently.

This is fascinating to do and can change one's self concept.

There is, however, no need to short change yourself; go for the genius factor, that alignment of the conscious mind and the energy mind, when the two become more than the sum of their parts and we really do get to think, feel and experience at a level few people ever even dream of experiencing.

Improve Your Genius Factor

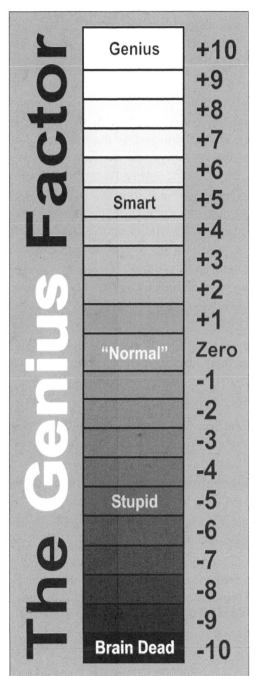

Here is a simple method, using a version of the SUE scale to firstly, determine your Genius Factor, and secondly, improve upon it with EFT.

Touch the scale with your fingertip and feel for "where you are at, right now," as far as genius is concerned.

Now do a round of EFT simply with the set up of, "Genius."

Pay attention to your body sensations; if you get a strong sensation in any part of your body during this round, use the EFT Body Protocol to improve energy flow there.

You might also get memories pop up; make a note of any memories relating to being a genius, being a creative genius and/or being highly intelligent and treat those with the EFT Story Protocol.

Being really intelligent and in full possession of your natural wits on every level is a good thing and extremely useful; it can even be life saving.

Keep working on your Genius Factor until it really is at +10 - that's your natural genius, you were born to experience that, and all you are doing is to finally claim your birthright of being a proper, fully functioning human being.

Genius In Every Day

How "genius" you get to be absolutely depends on how energized your are at any time; likewise, when your energy gets disturbed or very low, you get to be "stupid" in direct correlation.

Removing major blocks to accessing our natural genius is one thing; but learning to be a genius and stay a genius takes more.

You need to pay attention to your ongoing energy situation. It really helps at the beginning to carry the SUE scale around with you, or the Genius Factor scale, and check *before* you make decisions where you are, right here, right now.

The fact that a person can be super intelligent at 9.30 in the morning, and five minutes later do something incredibly stupid and damaging has confused people probably more than any other type of human behaviour in the past.

When we take the energy system into consideration, of course it makes sense - something happened to our super intelligent person at some time between 9.30 and 9.35 to cause them stress, their energy system went haywire and now they're in "stupid town."

- *Every person* **is going to be very intelligent and very stupid, many times, every day, as their energy system reacts to what's going on around them.**

This includes you and me, to be sure.

It includes children, old people, even learning disabled people have their own individual scale with their own personal, unique +10, which is the best they can possibly function.

If we want access to our best intelligence, our personal genius, we need to pay attention to where we're at energetically at any given point in time.

What is also very important to understand is that genius isn't just for brain surgeons, physicists and pure mathematicians.

When a friend comes in with a problem on their mind, we might need a genius idea what to say to them to make them feel better, for example. To take a moment out to de-stress and bring up the Genius Factor at such times can lead to truly transformational experiences.

There are so many times and places where genius ideas, genius thinking and genius solutions come in handy for real everyday life, for real every day people, such as mothers and fathers, grandmothers and grandfathers, friends, wives, husbands, colleagues, bricklayers, teachers, therapists, taxi drivers - every human being can do with a dose of genius to make life more exciting and a whole lot more fun.

If you use EFT for a time very specifically to bring up your personal genius factor, your energy system starts to wake up and often, you only need to think, "Genius!" and you can feel tension drain away, the lights getting brighter as your thinking clears, becomes more expansive and new ideas will come to you.

The Genius Factor is a very important aspect of using EFT and energy work to quite literally transform our lives, no matter what it is we are doing; we recommend this particularly highly as a core pattern to improve on just about everything we can conceive of, and to discover new solutions that were quite inconceivable before.

EFT & Goals

EFT can be used most wonderfully to remove, quite practically, the walls and blocks that stand between us now, and reaching that goal in the future.

EFT can also help us avoid chasing the wrong goals - and thus potentially saving our entire incarnation. Many people pursue goals all their life, only to find out on their death bed that they were engaged in a wild goose chase, a fool's errant, and it was the wrong goal all along.

This is so common and so wide spread that many intelligent and intuitive people refuse to set goals in the first place, for fear that they might be the wrong goals and take them away from their true life's path.

With EFT, we can consider all manner of goals, tap on them, and let the emotional entanglements fall away. When that happens, true goals become revealed, become empowered, and with that, our motivation and energy to go for goals that really matter rises exponentially.

Discovering New Goals

If the thought of goals and goal setting causes your stress levels to rise, treat this first. Good goals are good! They are motivational and a wonderful way in which we can steer our incarnation.

Simply imagine that you can have anything you want. It's all good, this is the starting point. Make a list of goals in the spirit of a young child, making their list for Father Christmas. You do not have to worry about any of these wants and needs to be remotely achievable; all you need to do is want this.

Over the top of the list, write:

"This is what I want in my life."

Keep writing, and when you can't think of anything else, look back at the headline, perhaps tap a round of Mindful EFT, and then add more topics and goals to your list.

You can keep adding to the list over a number of days, as more and other goals spring to mind.

Now, tap through the list, one item at a time.

You will find that some goals lose their sparkle and intensity; those are the false goals which were only on the list because of some kind of emotional/energetic entanglement. Tap a few more rounds of EFT on those so they are really gone and fully resolved, and you feel real emotional freedom from those.

Other goals become stronger, feel more powerfully attractive, "righter" and better, the more you tap on them.

Those are your true goals; and when you have found those, put them on a new list of goals.

Each one on this list should be very exciting to you, and you should feel a strong and powerful motivation to obtain the goal as soon as possible.

Step Stones To The Goal

Pick a goal and write it on the top of a fresh sheet of paper.

Now, write down the steps your future aspects will have to take to achieve the goal.

Make it clear and specific, precise and leave nothing out that is important.

When the list of steps to be taken is complete, use EFT to tap on every one of those steps until you have a high positive SUE scale reading on each one, at least +8 but preferably +10 on each one.

To achieve our true goals in life, we need energy!

We need the energy of excitement and the joy of working towards our goals; in short, we need to really love what we're doing to guarantee eventual success.

A tip: You don't have to tap through all the steps at the beginning. You can tap on the first step and start taking that step to get going towards the goal.

Come back to your list and tap the next step, and the next, until the path to the goal isn't just free and clear, but a powerful pathway, filled with energy, like a conveyor belt that will power you along towards your goal.

This is a wonderful way to work towards goals with EFT.

There is one more advantage to using EFT for achieving true life goals, and this is to deal with "what life throws at you."

When we start out on our path towards the goal, we can't predict exactly what is going to happen. Sometimes and for a variety of reasons, things can go wrong, stuff happens, plans go awry.

But with EFT on our side, that doesn't matter.

Even significant set backs which in the past would have literally "derailed" people from the path to their goal can be put into perspective, learned from and treated with EFT so we remain powerful, empowered and right on track towards the goal.

Combined with keeping an eye on general stress levels and making sure you remain positively energized, no matter what you have to do, and goal setting and goal achieving with EFT becomes a whole new experience.

EFT & Hypnosis

There are many ways in which EFT can be used to enhance and empower the processes of hypnosis, which seem so mysterious if we don't take the energy realms into consideration.

The first thing to do for anyone involved with hypnosis, be they a hypnotist, a hypnotherapist, a hypnosis client or a practitioner of self hypnosis, is to deal with their "hypnosis blockages and reversals."

Because of the peculiar effects, dubious reputation and mysterious ways of hypnosis, there is a great deal of fear and uncertainty around the whole topic; this is not a clean white thoughtfield by any means and everyone who comes into contact with it will experience energetic disturbances because of that.

So the first order of the day is to "clean the topic" by simply doing a few EFT treatment rounds on "Hypnosis!" as the set up, with the reminder phrase of, "Hypnosis!"

As you carefully and mindfully go through the EFT treatment round, pay attention to your body sensations (emotions) and any memories that flash up relating to the topic of hypnosis.

Now we can make a list of topics, including:

- Beliefs and limiting beliefs about hypnosis, hypnotists and trance;
- Past hypnosis/trance related traumas;
- Past related positive events, Guiding Stars, we got stuck on;
- Entrainments about hypnosis from society, religion, science or study;
- Personal worries, fears or other types of negative emotions;
- Questions and unresolved issues relating to the practice of hypnosis.

Every one of these denotes some kind of blockage in the energy system and we will be much better off without them.

This is particularly important for practising hypnotists and hypnotherapists who often don't perform anywhere near their own true optimal power levels, which is something they have in common with healers and other holistic practitioners across the board.

EFT For Hypnotists

The reversals relating to the Svengali archetype of the whirly eyed, all powerful puppet master hypnotist is the core problem for everyone who works as a hypnotist today. Whether there is strong rejection to the mesmeric archetype as being horrible, unconscionable and evil, or whether someone wholeheartedly embraces it and "hungers" for that kind of mind control power over their hapless victims, either way, that's a massive blockage which needs to go.

A good set up to get started on this topic is "Hypnosis power," or "My hypnosis powers," and work with it until you get to the +10 on the SUE scale. This will bring up personal blockages and reversals so that these may be resolved. Interestingly, for most hypnotists who work with this set up it tends to evolve to "personal power," and then just "power" at the end.

Professional hypnosis has many components and skills; we can use EFT to bring up those which are perhaps not as well expressed as they might be and raise the ceiling on the aspects of the hypnotic process we are already very good at.

As is the case with healers, entering the state of "I am the hypnotist," prior to meeting with clients by doing a few rounds of EFT to bring the SUE level on the topic to a +10 is a fascinating thing to do and changes the nature of what happens next, as it must.

A re-energizing and clearing round of EFT after a client leaves also makes a huge difference, especially in the long run.

EFT In The Hypnosis Treatment Flow

EFT can be used in many ways in the flow of a hypnosis or hypnotherapy session.

The most important and most valuable contribution is to use EFT to de-stress the client before an induction. Doing a few rounds of EFT for general stress together with the client, both tapping on stress at the same time, will lead to a calmer and more hypnosis-ready client and practitioner; and it will also greatly assist the process of getting into rapport.

Fears and worries the client might have about the hypnotic process can also be addressed at this time.

When the client is in trance and the hypnotic induction is in progress, the hypnotist can proxy tap for the client as they go through the induction.

This is a very powerful thing to do and with experience, a hypnotist can "take out" blockages that arise during certain parts of the induction.

After the induction, a round of EFT to bring up energy levels to a high positive on the SUE scale makes sure the client really is fully awake, has had a good experience and takes away an additional self help tool they can use at home to support the benefits of the hypnosis session from their end.

EFT & Hypnosis Programs

The experience of recorded hypnosis and guided meditation programs can be significantly enhanced for the home user.

Here is a sequence to help you get the most out of your hypnosis recordings.

- Start by taking the actual hypnosis tape, CD or if a digital product, the product image on a computer screen and do a round of Mindful EFT first. This cleans out any shields and blockages to the program which can get in the way of gaining as much as possible from its use.

- On the first listening, stay upright and awake and tap along to the program, paying close attention to the feelings in your body.

- If you come across any ZZZTs - moments that jar or words or suggestions that cause a negative response - stop the recording and treat that ZZZT with EFT. Rewind and test if the ZZZT has gone and now the recording can be received smoothly and easily.

- Go through the entire program this way so you know what is being said and there are no ZZZTs left. This will help you relax immensely more and enter much more profound states of trance because the worry about what's happening has been released completely.

- Before you enter into the program fully for the first time, first do a round or two of EFT on "Stress." Releasing general stress before going into a hypnotic trance allows you to go deeper/higher faster.

- Then do a round of EFT to affirm that you want to use this program for your personal evolution, and that you're ready and willing to participate fully in the process from your end. This can be as simple as tapping on, "I want confidence," with the reminder phrase of "Confidence!" if the hypnosis program relates to "Confidence," for example.

- Now settle down and enter into the hypnosis program from this whole new place. You will find your results with hypnosis programs improve tremendously, as does your personal enjoyment of the trance processes which are always fascinating and very enlivening.

- After the program is over, do a round of EFT for something that's appropriate to how you're feeling now, a positive energy flow round so you are fully energized, wide awake and ready for action.

By using EFT, we can unlock the tremendous power and support that is available in modern hypnosis programs - a world of extraordinary experiences awaits!

EFT & Illness

EFT doesn't "cure" any physical illness as it works not on the physical body, but the energy body instead.

However, if we can keep the energy body strong and flowing powerfully, we can change the experience of illness profoundly. We also alleviate stress on the system overall and thus can give the body the best conditions to be able to go about healing and restoring itself.

The body, left to its own devices, has immensely powerful self healing systems which never cease to strive and repair damage, right up until the very end. There was a case of a very elderly lady who had been mugged and stabbed; the police had to find out if she died during the stabbing, or later, in order to field the right charges against the perpetrator. This lady was over ninety years old and had died in an alleyway in winter; and yet the medical examiner could tell that she lived on for some hours after the attack because her skin had already started to heal itself again.

 Giving the body the space it needs to do its job and not getting in the way with additional disturbances is the big task of a person who has any kind of illness.

Self Help EFT & Illness

A person may feel helpless or that they can't do anything, that their life is in the hands of physicians or other carers now and all they can do is lie there and worry, but if we consider the energy system as well, there are many things we can do to help our physical bodies at time of illness.

The first is to reduce stress on the energy system and pay attention to the emotions that tell us we need to take some action.

A first step is simply to de-stress, as always. By focusing on energy body stress first we get to the most important treatment places in the energy system as directly as possible.

Using the EFT Body Protocol, we can ask, "Where do I feel this illness most in my body?" and make a set up from the physical sensations, including pain if that is involved in the illness.

It is particularly important not to stop too soon and keep tapping until positive feeling emerge - feelings of warmth, or love, or comfort in the places that were previously uncomfortable.

This indicates that good, healthy energy flow is now happening and this is very important indeed.

Also, in an ongoing illness, this is a treatment which needs to be repeated to keep the channels open and the energy flowing cleanly.

We can also use the Loving Touch Protocol during illness which can be very soothing and helpful.

- **If a person is very ill and has little energy left to do any EFT, we recommend the simple Heart Healing posture as something that can still be done.**

Here, what energy there is is focused on the Heart Centre, the most important part of the energy body, to help give it strength. This is very stabilising and together with the Loving Touch EFT Protocol is the furthest end of still being able to do something ourselves when we are very ill.

Three Lines Of Enquiry

Before we start to investigate and treat illness of any kind with EFT, we always want to start by tapping a round or two of EFT on general "stress." This calms down mind, body and spirit, we can think more clearly and that makes it much easier to formulate a good set up statement.

When we are ready, we can consider these.

Line of Enquiry 1: Thoughts

Use set up statements relating to thoughts about and awareness of the disease:

"My blood pressure is too high ...," - "I suffer from ..." , "I have (insert name of illness) ..." etc.

Line of Enquiry 2: Events

Use set up statements relating to the timeline of events, i.e. what happened just before the onset of the illness and which may be energetically related to the physical problem.

"I lost my job ..." - "My husband came back from Iraq ..." - "My mother died ..." - "The doctor said ...." etc.

These are very powerful approaches to helping illness with EFT as EFT is all about dealing with the energy body problems, not the physical problems.

Line of Enquiry 3: Feelings

Use set up statements relating to the actual feelings about the illness, the emotions caused by the illness.

"I can't believe I have (x)" - "I am terrified of my (x)" - "I feel terribly sad because I have (x)" - "I hate my (x)."

To release our emotional entanglements with the disease or illness is extremely beneficial and really helps the body relax and stand a better chance of fighting the illness.

If you are the patient, start with the line of enquiry that seems the most urgent or important to you; if you are a practitioner, you can offer the choice of the three lines of enquiry to the client, or take them through all three, one session at a time, in the order you deem best.

As you tap through the set up statements generated by the three lines of enquiry, quite a bit of experience and practice builds up and after having worked with all three, a very rounded and holistic treatment, but also a new understanding of the disease begins to emerge.

Importantly however, this simply model of the 3 Lines Of Enquiry gives people a place to start tapping EFT in the first place - which is the most important event of them all. So ask:

- What do I think?
- What has happened to me?
- How do I feel about this right now?

.. and the answers you give are the first set ups that will take you to the heart of the problem.

Illness & Energy Tonics

Energy EFT is never just about tapping our bad feelings away; it is about improving the flow of energy through the energy body as often as we can.

Especially when we are ill, we need additional energies to help our energy bodies stay strong, and to provide the energetic backbone to the mind, body, spirit system that is engaged in the all important task of self healing.

We can give the energy body much needed "energy tonics" by tapping EFT for positive energy forms; and we can get the right energy forms by simply asking ourselves, "What do I really need and want to feel right now?" The answer to that question gives us the EFT set up and is the first step to re-energizing ourselves in personal way.

Thinking about what we do need and what would make us happier, stronger, feel better is also a good antidote to always getting stuck in thinking about our problems.

Here is list of positive energy forms[4] we can tap on to encourage positive, nourishing and revitalising energy flow:

Abundance	Home	Space
Admiration	Hope	Stillness
Angel	Immortality	Strength
Beauty	Inspiration	Success
Blessings	Joy	Sunshine
Brilliance	Kindness	Surprise
Clarity	Lifting	Tenderness
Confidence	Lightness	Time
Creativity	Logic	Tranquillity
Diversity	Love	Transformation
Dominion	Luck	Treasures
Energy	Magic	Truth
Evolution	Mystery	Union
Excitement	Peace	Unknown
Festival	Play	Vision
Fortune	Power	Vitality
Freedom	Pride	Wealth
Grace	Purpose	Wisdom
Happiness	Resonance	Wonderment
Harmony	Sanctuary	Youth
Health	Satisfaction	
Holy	Serenity	

Taking good care of the energy body is something we can all do for ourselves; it is really important to all the processes of physical healing and can give us a positive focus in ill health, sickness and disease.

This may not always immediately improve our health or make illnesses disappear mysteriously; but it is the right thing to do and most importantly, will transform our experience of illness with the power of energy EFT.

---

4   Positive Energy Essences from "For You, A Star" Hartmann 2004

EFT & Intuition

Thanks to modern energy work, we have finally discovered that intuition is feeling the real feelings in the body which have no physical reason - it is the expression of movements in the energy body transmitted through sensations.

Intuition really is the "gut instinct" that "tells us" information which can't be seen, heard, smelled, tasted or touched.

These sensations do not only live in the "gut" but all over the body and each person experiences their intuition differently. A prickling in the back of the neck which tells of danger; a small shiver going down the spine that tells us something is going on; getting the sensation of feeling cold in a warm room, all of these are examples of intuition in action.

Intuition sensations can be drowned out by physical discomfort and by energy body stress; and although every person has this system of intuition, most people go through life and rarely notice these sensations that give us important additional information.

In order to improve our intuition awareness, we need to start paying attention to sensations in the body again.

The Mindful EFT Protocol is particularly good to help us reconnect to the body sensations, our 6th Sense.

As an exercise in improving intuition, go through a round of EFT and simply focus on what you can feel in your body as you tap each point slowly and for a little while.

Say nothing (no set up) and simply tap and scan your body, head to toe, to notice all the many small sensations, their locations, how they feel.

Becoming aware of these 6th Sense sensations is the first step to be able to use intuition far more accurately and make good use of this additional information about the world.

Also, bear in mind that stress drowns out the signals from your natural intuition; making sure you decrease energy body stress often, but particularly when it comes to making important decisions, so you can become aware of your intuition and let it help guide you correctly.

- **Intuition is another word for using the 6th sense, feeling energy in the body.**

EFT & Learning

People are born veritable learning machines and as long as they remain reasonably healthy, will continue to have the potential to learn at a rapid rate - unless there are blocks to learning.

Working with EFT, we can significantly enhance the experience of learning in every sense. Then we learn more, learn more deeply, enjoy learning and will be able to retain and use what we have learned as well at a whole new level.

In 2009, we took the unprecedented step to make it a requirement for all AMT distance learning courses that the student should be "energy enabled."

This allows the authors of the courses to present more content more quickly; to present more complex and in-depth material and to set much more difficult exercises right from the start. Being able to use EFT to expedite their studies so significantly improves the performance and the experience of the students, we felt we could no longer go on without this.

Amongst the observed effects of EFT on the students were:

- **General reduction in "study stress" and more enjoyment of the courses.**

Many of the students, all adults from a wide variety of educational backgrounds and from many different countries, a significant proportion of whom had English as a second language, used EFT to overcome performance pressure, feeling pressured by time, previous learning traumas and limiting beliefs around learning. .

- **Greatly reduced procrastination.**

Procrastination, or the refusal to engage in something that is perceived as painful or frightening in some way, was previously the No. 1 reason for students not finishing the courses on time or failing to hand in assignments. EFT essentially puts an end to procrastination. Just a few rounds on the "good reasons" why we can't start to do the assignments, right away, and the students turn from procrastination to actually wanting to interact with the course material.

- **Easier and more rapid absorption of written material.**

In general, when the student doesn't understand something, they read it again, out aloud, slowly whilst tapping. With the triple action of de-stressing as well as removing blocks and re-energizing, the students often report improved clarity, as well as improved depth of comprehension. This has also reduced the amount of additional help the tutors have to provide as often, a round of EFT is all the student needed to be able to understand the material.

- **Better expression and communication from the students.**

Being able to express one's ideas fluently and coherently also improves tremendously when the student is less stressed, and is able to address specific personal problems with EFT. For example, a student for whom English was the second language tapped on his fears to not be able to "find the right words." This was a -7 on the SUE scale, so quite a big fear which would have had a significant effect on his ability to think straight. He tapped until he got it down to 0, then continued to tap the same set up, "The right words will come to me," until he felt really positive and energized. Needless to say, his communication and confidence improved significantly and he passed the course with top grades.

- **Better relationships with the tutors.**

Less stressed students performing better naturally leads to a much better relationship with the tutors, more good feedback from the tutors, more good marks given. This produces a far more positive, learning focused atmosphere and instead of study stress, there is excitement about the learning process for both tutor and student.

- **Better retention of course materials and information.**

Studying with less stress and an attitude of enjoyment, curiosity and excitement about the materials being studied already naturally leads to a better understanding, better retention and recall. As one student said, "I am so surprised how much I've learned simply by not being so worried about my learning any more!" This then also reflects on:

- **Better test results.**

Using EFT for exam stress of course significantly improves test results across the board. Many people have all manner of blockages in their systems from bad experiences with education in the past, and to discover them and simply take them out with EFT leads to a much happier student and a completely different test experience. Also, being able to tap during the test itself should stress levels rise or a question seem daunting is a tremendous help to make retrieving information smooth and easy.

- **Better focus on the course overall.**

Being able to de-stress at will by using EFT allows students to work through the course, even when there are challenges and problems with their personal circumstances.

For example, one student who was going through a divorce in the middle of the course reported that sitting down to study and tapping a few rounds of EFT on their divorce stress before they started "created a wonderful clear space, an oasis in my day, and I loved every moment of it."

This is a good example for the kind of student who in the past would have dropped out and not finished the course at all, never mind with flying colours as this student did.

The ability of EFT to "unlock" the learning powers of a person of any age is so important, we should not reserve it for the classroom or study alone.

We live in an age where we are all constantly challenged to learn new things. Whether it is learning to use a new computer or a new telephone, learning new ways to replace old behaviours, learning from our experience, the more ready and willing we are to learn and the better we get at it, the better life tends to become.

EFT & Luck

J. B. Rhine, who began investigating paranormal phenomena at Duke University in 1927, conducted a series of experiments whereby volunteers had to predict a suit of cards from a choice of four. He conducted many experiments, and his data showed a small statistical anomaly but it wasn't enough to prove the existence of extra sensory perception.

Recently, someone looked at his raw data and noticed that there were some test results that were so bad, they were statistically significant also. There had been people who got absolutely nothing right, or much less than their "fair share" of accidental good luck. If you add those people, the ones who somehow managed to defy the odds and never get lucky to the ones who nearly always got lucky, you do end up with a really significant result for Rhine's experiments.

Theoretically, everyone should "get lucky" some of the time. On the toss of a coin, there is a 50% chance each time to get it right, and the more often this is repeated, the more "luck" averages out towards that 50/50 middle of the road result.

- **If there is no factor X involved we would all be 50% lucky over time.**

Yet we know that this isn't so. From our life's experiences we know that some people are far more lucky than others.

This goes from wining raffles, tombolas, at the gambling table, betting on horses and such to much broader and wider luck related concepts - finding yourself in the right place at the right time, lucky co-incidences, lucky escapes, lucky in love ...

Were you born under a lucky star?

Do you get at least your fair share of the random luck that should be on offer for everyone?

If you feel that the answer to this is, "No, actually, I don't ..." we may begin to wonder what blockages we might have in our systems that stop us from being at least as lucky as the next fellow, at least over time.

So sit back and think about luck in your life, across the time of your life, and to find some good personal set ups for EFT treatments to improve the flow of luck in your life.

Finding Set Ups For Luck

- What is luck? What does luck and being lucky mean to you?

- Would you like to be lucky?

- How important is it to have Lady Luck on your side?

- How do you feel about taking a chance, betting, taking risks?

- Could it be you are amongst those who will say, when someone wishes them, "Good luck!" immediately hold up a hand, deflect the incoming energy and say, "I don't need it! I do everything by hard work, it's more reliable!"

- Or perhaps you thought you were lucky once, but then something happened and your "luck has left you"?

- How do you feel about relying on luck as something that is absolutely necessary for success?

- Do you need help with your luck, such as owning a lucky rabbits foot and when that gets lost, the luck disappears with it?

- Can a person "make their own luck"?

- How do you feel about the idea that there are such things as "lucky streaks"

- Or that luck is a finite commodity that will "run out" if you use it all up too soon?

- Was there ever a time when you pinned your hopes on luck, and it let you down?

- Does the religion of your childhood have something to say about luck and who gets to have it?

- Compared to the luckiest person you know, how lucky are you?

Lift Your Luck Factor

The LUCK Factor

Blessed	+10
	+9
	+8
	+7
	+6
Lucky	+5
	+4
	+3
	+2
	+1
50/50 Chance	Zero
	-1
	-2
	-3
	-4
Unlucky	-5
	-6
	-7
	-8
	-9
Doomed	-10

"On a scale of -10 to +10, +10 being unbelievably lucky, constantly lucky, and -10 never having any luck of any kind whatsoever, how lucky are you, right here and now?"

Put your fingertip on the scale and slide it along until you can feel a click - "Yes, that's right, this number is my luck factor."

Now do a round of EFT on "I'm lucky!" with the reminder phrase of, "Lucky me!"

Check the scale and get your next reading.

Continue until you are on the positive side, and then change the set up to "I'm very lucky," and "All the luck in the world!" with the reminder phrase of simply, "Luck" to take it really high up to +8 at least.

Now, if you were to rush out to a casino, would you be guaranteed to win?

This we cannot know; but what we do know is that "luck" isn't just about card tricks, far from it; and to take out blockages of any kind in our energy system is always a very good thing indeed.

With your luck factor restored and luck energy running free and high, there is then also the question of, "And what can happen next ...?"

189

EFT & Meditation

Meditation has been proven, time and time again, to relieve stress and allow people to lead happier, healthier lives.

But here's the rub - stressed people find it very difficult if not entirely impossible to "calm their mind" and start with the processes of meditation!

The very people who need it the most can't meditate but worry no longer, here comes EFT to the rescue.

When the energy flow in our systems becomes smooth, lively and enlivening, we start to think far more clearly and find entering states of expansive and truly wonderful meditation not just easy, but natural and very simple to do.

Try this out for yourself.

On the SUE scale, how stressed are you right now? The worse the stress, the lower the negative number. Slide your finger over the scale to help you gain a sense of "where you are at" right now.

Make a mental note of the number, and now try to imagine you are walking on the shores of an ocean, white sand, blue sky, tropical trees to the right and wonderful turquoise white crested waves to the left.

Now, tap a round of EFT with the set up of, "Relax ..."

Remember to breathe deeply in and out on each point and say the word "Relaaaax ..." on the out breath.

When you are done, go back to the beach and notice how much more "present" you are now, how much more "real" walking on the beach has become.

You may also notice that you can now feel more, spray from the water perhaps, hear sea birds and waves, scent the ocean air - our senses start to unfold when we de-stress and our whole body, energy body and mind begin to respond to being on a beach that isn't here and yet, we are there.

Startling out of meditations such as the walk along the beach is always a sign that you are still too stressed and you need to relax much, much more. Also, pay attention to your energy flow. Relaxing down to the Zero point in the SUE scale causes you to become drowsy; and this in turn causes people to fall asleep rather than to experience lucid, living meditations that are so immensely healing for mind, body and spirit.

Tap an extra round of EFT or two to really improve your energy flow to the positive side of the SUE scale and then try the beach walk again.

Even if you can only get a flashing sense of really being there, you have now an idea of what you are aiming for - entering into an autogenic reality where you can think, feel, be and do anything you want to make you happier in the widest metaphorical sense.

Using EFT to de-stress before meditating is a wonderful way to unlock the power of meditating (and also hypnosis and self hypnosis) - it's a life skill, and highly recommended indeed.

EFT & Memories

When we are working with the energy body and treating what are in fact energy body memories, the disturbances which still exist in the energy body and cause malfunctions today, we take a different approach to memories.

We do not make any distinction between a "real" memory, a hallucination, a dream, a false memory, a vivid imagining, a past life memory or a drug induced memory; we simply take the tack that if a person experiences something as highly disturbing, frightening, painful or relevant to the problem at hand, it denotes an energy body disturbance and we can treat it with EFT, regardless where it came from.

In modern energy work we are not particularly concerned with the content of a memory, details about who did what to whom, when, where or how many times; what concerns us is how the person is feeling today, here and now, and to make them feel better.

In the course of treating all kinds of memories with EFT, memories become clearer and more accessible when energy flow improves towards the positive end of the SUE scale. This is a natural process that always happens when we remove disturbances and improve energy (information[5]) flow in the energy system.

As always, but particularly when we are dealing with memories in that wide sense as defined above, we want to de-stress and re-energize before we start.

General energy body stress and particular energy body stress relating to the emotions of the memory makes memory recall very difficult; the stress de-stabilises the whole memory retrieval system and causes confused, mixed up memory data that we can't consciously make sense of.

For EFT treatments to work, we do not have to remember details.

We can use the EFT Body Protocol to focus on our feelings today about whatever it was that happened back then, and tap on those instead. This is a veritable God sent for people who suffer with so called re-pressed memories or have the feeling that "something" happened, but they don't know what or when.

To learn how to work with your own memories in self help first before dealing with disturbing or particularly powerful memories is a very good idea.

---

5   See "EmoTrance: Emotions, Energy, Information & Love" Hartmann 2011

It is also important to stop chasing trauma and only ever focusing on traumatic memories only; trauma events represent only 25% of the reasons why we do the things we do (see *Four Types of Events* in the *EFT & Events* Section).

For practice, remember some good childhood memories and write them down using the EFT Story Protocol. Do a round of EFT, step by step, to strongly re-connect with the positive memory and improve energy flow to a real high on the SUE scale, +8 and above.

In doing this, you learn how better energy flow improves the memory, makes it clearer, brighter and you can feel it more strongly; there are also always lessons for us now in the process of doing a little energy work with memories.

This is highly recommended as an exercise; and the more important bad memories and trauma appear to be in your life, the more important it is to balance that trauma quest with accessing good memories in equal measure. It is easy to consciously come to the conclusion that "My life is terrible!" if one focuses on nothing but trauma for a few decades to the exclusion of all else. Real trauma is a lightning strike; and so it is for good memories. We are not looking for long stretches of time but certain moments when life was good, wonderful, or we were simply awed and amazed by something.

Another interesting and useful set of exercises for EFT and memory work is to make a list of school memories that stand out - good memories, bad memories, slightly embarrassing memories, and fun memories too. Put them into your EFT treatment bowl and tap on them as and when you feel like it.

This is excellent practice, very informative, and not only do we learn a lot about our lives and our aspects across time, but we also significantly improve energy flow in the energy body which is quite timeless in its own way, and where all of these things still exist.

Once you feel that you are familiar with how EFT works for you, confident in your ability to keep your stress down and yourself energized, clear and ready for action, and you have built up some experience, you can consider going to some of the more difficult memories as well.

In general, if you can think of working with EFT that you are not dealing with memories in the psychology sense, but actually existing structures in your own energy system, working with memories across the board becomes logical and doable.

EFT & Metaphors

Metaphors - descriptions of things that are not "here" in the physical world - have long confused people on so many levels.

Nowadays, we say that metaphors are a translation of energy existences in a person's energy field, and they are generated by the energy mind, the head of the energy body (previously known as the sub- or unconscious mind).

When we use EFT, we do not need to concern ourselves with linguistic contortions or mental convolutions when it comes to metaphor - we simply take it and tap on it with a view to evolve it, make it better than it was.

For example, there was a lady who always had a sore throat and described this by saying, "I feel like there's a piece of holly stuck in my throat!"

There is no physical holly in her throat, clearly; we are talking about a metaphorical description of some kind of energy thing (erea) that got stuck in her throat at some time.

Using the set up of, "Holly in my throat," and the reminder phrase of "Holly," the lady reported that it started to soften and felt more like jelly after the first round.

This became the set up for the next round, "Jelly in my throat," with the reminder phrase of, "Jelly."

She then said that in the middle of the round, the jelly started to slide down into her stomach, which felt weird and made her slightly sick. The next round was for "Jelly in my stomach," and at the end of this EFT round, she started to smile and say, "It feels fine now - and my throat feels really nice, first time in years I feel like I can breathe, speak ... this is great, I feel great!"

The trick with metaphor is to not get hung up on "what it might mean" but simply treat the metaphor at face value, and tap on it.

Here's another example.

A young gentleman talked about a pressure on his head, "like a steel helmet pressing in on my brain." He happened to be a soldier; but when we use EFT with metaphor, we really must abstain from drifting off into psychoanalysis and stick with the metaphor as we make our set ups. This "takes the metaphor seriously" and treats exactly what's wrong, instead of a whole lot of things that might or might not be relevant to the problem in hand, which in this case, were serious migraines.

The set up therefore was, "The steel helmet pressing in on my brain," with "steel helmet" as the reminder phrase.

After the first round, the steel helmet had become both softer and larger; now it felt more like "wearing a soft turban, quite nice, actually."

Another round on the "soft turban" had this young man saying, "It feels like swirling confusion, I want to unwrap the turban, I want a clear head!"

"Clear head" took the feelings to the positive side of the SUE scale, and at the end, the young man was laughing and saying he had not felt so clear and free in his head - ever.

When we work with energy and EFT, working with metaphors and evolving them forward to a solution and a Healing Event is really simple and easy. Not just that, in so many cases it is the most direct route to solving an energy problem that would be impossible to treat in any other way.

Metaphors Of Life

Another time when using metaphor can be very helpful in EFT treatments is when the problem is so great or so complicated, it could generate a virtually infinite number of potential set ups and we could conceivably be tapping forever.

An older lady, Thelma, had lost both her husband and her son due to a car accident. She was also about to lose her home as she could no longer afford to live there, which meant giving up her beloved horses and a garden she had been taking care of for many years. Her health was failing on many fronts, and on top of everything else, she had fallen and broken her leg in three places recently.

When asked the question, "If you life was a place in time and space, what would it be?" she answered, "It is a frozen desert where nothing grows, hard rocks, black, frozen ground, nothing moves, just an icy wind that sucks all the life out of everything."

This description is "how it is" and as with all EFT treatments, we want to bring more energy into this system to allow it to move forward, to evolve.

The first set up was, "This frozen desert," with "frozen" for the reminder phrase.

After the first round, Thelma sighed and said, "This place is stuck in forever night," which was the set up for the next round. After this round she sighed again, started to move around a little, stretched her neck and rotated her shoulders. She reported that in the frozen world, the wind had died down and it was quieter now, a little less cold.

She said, "It feels like there might be a chance that some time, winter could turn to spring, the sun might return."

The next set up was, "The sun might return," with the reminder phrase of, "the sun."

During this round, Thelma started to cry and said, "I so wish the sun would come back, bring life again, life is waiting for the sun."

"Life is waiting for the sun," became the next set up and after this round, Thelma said, "This is amazing! I can feel the sun getting stronger, and there are little tiny blades of grass amongst the rock! Life is returning!"

By the time the session ended, the land was warming under the life giving rays of the sun, grass was growing, some small flowers and even seedlings of trees had begun to show themselves. There were also small animals and insects, "life was really starting to return."

By staying fully focused on the metaphorical land, Thelma had managed to feel a sense of aliveness and a beginning return of "a kind of inner strength I thought I'd lost for good."

This is an example of foundational and really soothing energy work that can give people hope and more importantly, the energy to move forward and perhaps tap on more specific problems related to her losses and experiences in the future.

This kind of "global metaphor energy intervention" can be as simple as to ask of a person, "If your problem was a place in time and space, what kind of place would it be?" and then tap to improve the land, a little further on each round. Extremely fascinating and empowering on so many levels.

EFT & Money

How much money a person can earn is directly linked to how stressed or afraid they are.

This has been summed up by saying that "how much money you can earn is directly proportional to your ability to do the things that need to be done in order to make the money you want to make."

People simply do not do those things "which need to be done" because they are stressed, blocked or reversed against doing them, whatever they may be.

For example, one gentleman wasn't getting promoted because he was thought to be "not leadership material." This was because he wasn't putting himself forward as a team leader when the occasions arose, wasn't standing up to give presentations, and didn't give voice to his ideas.

He described himself as "being very uncomfortable" in such situations and preferring to do work quietly by himself. We can also call this "being afraid" of doing those things (which needed to be done to get a promotion and earn more money) or we can simply say, "Those are energy reversals. Let's tap EFT on them, take them out, improve the gentleman's energy flow and confidence, and clear the path towards that promotion!"

Another gentleman wasn't progressing on his career path because the next step involved additional accreditation, studying, tests and theory exams. He said that he "was a practical guy and not interested in book stuff," and we might say that he was afraid of taking on the study and the tests, or that he had some energy reversals we can treat with EFT.

Then there was a lady who had a reasonable career but there was a definite ceiling beyond which the career path didn't stretch. In order to get more money, she would have to leave her safe but boring and relatively low paid job altogether and find a different line of work, more suited to her talents and ambitions. For many years she thought about it but could never quite make the move; the thought of "leaping into the unknown" scared her too much. Working with EFT firstly reduced her fears and worries, then gave her the confidence and clarity to take action. Sensibly, she found herself a new job before leaving the old one; so the move was entirely without trauma, the right thing to do and she said, "I wish to God I had EFT ten years ago!"

A lady therapist with a struggling practice used EFT to get herself to do those things she knew needed to be done in order to get more and better paying clients, but which she had failed to do for years. Some of these, such as keeping good records, vigorous advertising and calling her clients had been deemed to be "beneath her" and "taking her away from her real passion which was working with clients." A few rounds of EFT later and she realised that these were only justifications; she had been afraid and stress blocked against those essential activities. With the blocks out of the way, she started doing those things that needed to be done, and of course, the results spoke for themselves.

We all have our own blockages in our energy systems; there is no shame in admitting that we are too afraid to cold call, find haggling for a better deal physically painful, think we can't do this or that because it would be too difficult, engage in procrastination and in general, shy away from a task that needs to be done like a skittish horse from a fence that seems to high to jump.

We also all do know what needs to be done; and the not doing it sets up an endless conflict which adds to stress and misery, day in, day out.

The more stressed we become, the worse our financial decision making gets as well. Stress reduces the ability to think clearly and to plan for the long term; it produces a kind of tunnel vision, and any thing that can alleviate the stress for a moment is embraced. Credit card companies with their ridiculous interest charges and operating procedures live on the fact that people are too stressed to think straight, and are thus willing to make any deal with any devil to get a few illusionary moments of relief.

Over time, this can lead a person into ever worsening money problems and ever worsening stress, which leads to even worse decisions ...

When we apply EFT to any situation, including the worst types of money situations, the very first thing that happens is that the fog of stress starts to disappear and we can think more clearly again.

This a good thing; and even the worst financial dire straits can be untangled and unravelled when stress has receded, some of the most frightening aspects have been dealt with with EFT and a measure of logic and reason has been regained.

A lady whose husband had died and whose income was not enough to keep up the family home had entered into numerous disastrous financial deals to somehow keep it all going. She described herself as "frozen, entirely unable to do anything, take control of anything, I knew it was all heading for disaster and I was getting sick with the stress but there was nothing I could do."

EFT helped her come out of that frozen state, and she realised then that she hadn't dealt with her husband's death emotionally. With the help of much EFT and a professional practitioner, she started to release the emotional hold on the house and was able to sell it. She was also able to get help and advice from debt agencies and when the process had taken its course, she had a new flat, regained control of her finances and had even found a promising career path, turning a favourite activity into her new profession.

Being able to undo deep emotional entanglements, setting people free in the true sense of Emotional Freedom, is one of the greatest gifts of EFT.

There are innumerable opportunities in the world to earn a good living; there is a flow of working and being rewarded for that. Money problems always arise when this flow is broken or blocked; and when we identify those blockages and treat them with EFT, financial logic can be regained.

An interesting example was a gentleman who had set his heart on being a professional musician, writing music, performing and selling his music. He was a classic "struggling artist," living below the breadline and rooming in with various friends and lovers and this had been going on for over a decade. His list of not doing the things that needed to be done included a proper website, getting up early in the mornings to chase leads and contact venues, self promotion and sorting out his various compositions for publication. It also included finding session work purely for the money so he would have some funds to invest in his own career. He started tapping EFT and reports that his big breakthrough came when he realised that "deep down, I didn't really believe in myself as a successful artist." When this block had been cleared with EFT, he said that not only did this completely change his focus, but all of a sudden he had so much more energy. The tasks that seemed so daunting before became easy, fun even. Not only did his financial situation improve, he also found that his compositions were now coming more frequently, were more powerful than they had ever been before, and he was finding "ever more joy in music itself."

Tips For Money & EFT

1. First of all, remember the stress and the effects it has on your logic, reason and emotions. The worse your money problems seem, the more important it is to de-stress on a regular basis and improve energy flow so you have the mental, physical and emotional strength to face your money challenges successfully.

2. Make a list of those "things that need to be done" and which you are currently not doing. Take your time and tap for one thing after the other, making sure each one is thoroughly resolved before you move on to the next.

3. TEST yourself against reality! It is not enough to be able to do those things that need to be done; keep tapping until you feel energized and you start to enjoy them, look forward to them, can't wait to start doing those things for real.

4. If scary feelings come back at any time, just stop and tap. It is always worth it and will stop you from making bad decisions or freezing up and doing nothing which is also very dangerous to your financial health.

5. Pay attention to money blocks and negative emotions relating to money in general as and when they occur in every day life. Money blocks reveal themselves when you get stressed or frightened, perhaps by a bill or a proposed meeting, by the thought of expenditure, or any thoughts and feelings during the day. Tap on these as soon as possible to regain a good "money flow" in your energy system.

6. If a past aspect has made bad decisions, undoubtedly due to stress and fear, it is time to forgive them. Use the EFT Proxy Protocol to tap on the aspect of you who (entered into that bad deal, lost the business, was too afraid to (x), didn't do (y), shouldn't have done (z), etc. etc.). Old money sins and money trauma are now only blocks in our energy systems and when we take them out, we feel so much better for it.

7. When we are fully energized, work turns into play. That's really true and you can experience this for yourself when you use EFT to improve the energy flow through your energy body. So we can use the very idea of "Oh no, this is going to be hard work!" as an indicator of an existing blockage and tap on it. It is amazing how quickly "hard work" turns into "well, that's not so bad ..." and then into, "Let me at it!"

In the past, it was thought that people who have financial problems have one or two major things wrong with them to cause this.

We have learned that it is ongoing, daily stress that disables people's logic and energy levels instead, and that this stress is cumulative over time.

When we really want to turn our money relationship around, we certainly want to address our biggest emotional problems, of course. But the real trick to long term financial success is to keep energy flowing every day and take out stress, blockages and reversals as soon as we become aware of them. Just as teeth need to be brushed every day to keep them clean, so our energy system needs to be cleaned of stress every day too.

A final tip: If money is a real source of stress and worry in your life, tap on it especially before going to bed, last thing at night. Keep tapping EFT until you feel deeply peaceful and ready to go into the night free of fears and worries. This will set you up for a better night's sleep and give you even more energy the next day to wake up and "do those things you know you need to do."

EFT & Pain

EFT & Physical Pain

Physical pain is a sign there's something wrong with the body, as emotional pain is the sign there's something wrong with the energy body.

As such, please make sure to seek the correct treatment forms and to go to a doctor to investigate the source of pain, always.

Having said that, when we tap EFT for physical pain, we often change the experience of pain in some way. By taking the energy body stress out of the equation, we give the body a chance to relax and physical healing can take place more easily. There is always merit in tapping EFT on all forms of physical pain.

A gentleman from the UK reports:

"I was awoken in the middle of the night by severe ear pain. It really was severe, unbearable, as bad as a toothache. I started tapping right away and quite frantically, and it didn't seem to do anything. But a few minutes later, when I found myself in the kitchen with a glass of water and a painkiller in one hand, and still tapping with the other, I realised that the EFT had taken the panic away and got me to the point where I remembered to take a pain killer!"

Many people have reported encouraging results with tapping EFT even for chronic pain. The dual action of relieving stress and feeling stronger, more energized in yourself is highly appreciated.

There are some areas of pain relief, however, where EFT really shines.

- **Phantom Pain:** The pain experienced after the loss of a limb has been reported to respond extremely well to the application of EFT.

- **Residual Pain:** Another type of pain that can disappear altogether by the application of EFT is recurring, residual pains from physical injuries that have healed well, for example after operations, broken bones and gunshot wounds.

EFT & Psychosomatic Pain

We have discovered that there exists a scale of emotions, physical feelings that come from the energy body and can be felt in the physical body.

The Emotion Range Scale:
All these are emotions, movements in the energy body that transmit to the physical body.

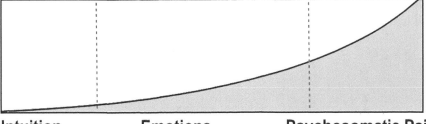

Intuition	Emotions	Psychosomatic Pain
Fine Sensations	Strong Sensations	Painful Sensations

At the lowest level are fine sensations that are termed "gut instinct," "intuition" and so forth.

When these sensations become stronger, we have what we normally call emotions.

When the sensations become even stronger, we run out of "emotion words" such as sadness or despair, and instead talk about feeling pain that is as strong as physical pain - psychosomatic pain, the high end form of emotions.

It is really important to treat psychosomatic pain as soon as possible as a breach into physical symptoms is imminent.

When the energy body is so damaged that it produces psychosomatic emotions that are indistinguishable from physical pain, it really becomes a possibility of a person "dying of a broken heart."

The best way to treat psychosomatic pain as well as all high end, physically noticeable emotions is to use the EFT Body Protocol.

A lady who had suffered multiple bereavements in a short period of time was suffering from a pain in the centre of her chest that felt like "a hard shard, like a piece of a sharp edged diamond cutting into me, all the time." Numerous physical examinations had found "nothing wrong" with her.

The first round of EFT had the set up of, "The hard shard in my chest," with the reminder phrase of "Shard." She reported that it felt a little softer, more like stone instead of diamond, which produced the next set up of, "This stone in my chest," with the reminder phrase of "stone."

Halfway through the round, the lady started to cry and said, "My heart has turned to stone," which became "This heaviness in my heart," which was a good evolution from the diamond hard shard we started with. Through further treatment rounds, the heaviness in the heart was lightened and love was sent particularly to the heart, with a set up of, "My loving heart."

The lady was then able to talk about her bereavements and said she felt ready to start on the healing process, as she now felt she was still alive, and still had much love to give before her own time ran out.

EFT & Performance

Problems with performance arise when stress becomes so great that a meltdown occurs, and then a person is no longer able to "perform."

This is complete performance failure; but many more people suffer from performance impairment, which means that they are not performing to the best of their abilities.

This is directly related to stress levels; the higher the stress, the more loss of performance occurs. This is energy body stress, made up of all manner of resonating emotions, which are movements of energy through the energy body; we can say that the more de-stabilised the energy system becomes, the more our performance is impaired across the board.

EFT is extremely efficient at removing energy body stress and by increasing the flow of energy through the energy body, we can turn stressful situations into feeling amazingly empowered and in full possession of all the many talents and abilities we have.

You might have noticed that nothing was said about what kind of performance we are dealing with here; sports performance, performance in bed, public speaking or singing, work performance, tests and exams or the many and varied ways and places stress can destabilise us.

This is because the relationship between stress and performance is so global and all-encompassing; the same principle applies across the board.

- **If you want to perform (at) anything the best you possibly can, your energy system needs to flow beautifully and you need to feel good inside.**

In tapping EFT for performance especially, it is really important to not just reduce the pain and fear of stress so you feel "nothing" - you need to keep tapping more rounds of EFT until you start to sparkle, feel inspired and not just ready to perform, but literally can't wait to do this thing.

To self treat performance anxiety, think about an example in the future where you will have to perform, and notice how this affects you as your stress levels rise.

- Notice how your breathing might have become faster, shallower, or stopped altogether.

- Notice the feelings in your body - where do you feel this stress the most as you think about having to perform?

- Notice how your thoughts start to jump and get jumbled - all this is simply just energy body stress.

- Now, take a deep breath, think about the future performance and just tap a round of EFT for "Stress."

- Pay attention to how you feel, think, breathe when the stress starts to recede.

- Keep thinking about that future performance and tap another round of EFT, again simply for "Stress!" with the reminder phrase of, "stress."

This is our first and most important step in improving any form of performance, namely to get ready to consider what is causing the most stress and to find the right set ups to remove your own personal performance stress once and for all.

Now, when you think about a future aspect of yourself who has to perform, what is the aspect most stressed about? What causes the aspect the most stress?

The answer to this question is your first set up for your EFT treatment round.

Use the SUE scale to find the negative number that describes how badly the future aspect is affected by this, and tap the round.

Check back with the SUE scale - how far has it moved towards the positive?

Keep tapping further rounds until when you think about that problem, not only has it gone completely but you feel good now, and your future aspect has also changed.

Now we can ask, "What else is causing the future aspect who has to perform stress?"

Repeat the sequence from above until when you think about the future aspect who has to perform you feel really happy and convinced now that they will be able to do really well.

Over the next few days, "check in with the aspect" every so often to make sure that nothing has been overlooked and the energy system has really been cleared out and is running smoothly.

Preparing For Performance With EFT

In the run up to the actual performance, keep an eye, ear and all your other feelers on your stress levels.

There may be other things which cause stress; and if there is a high background level of stress, any additional stress, such as you would expect for a performance, can be very de-stabilising.

For example, Richard's performance problem was about public speaking. But he was also under an immense amount of stress from problems with his relationship with his wife, who was threatening to divorce him and take the children.

When Richard tapped EFT for his future aspect who had to give an important presentation at work, he discovered that the aspect was so worried about his home situation, he was not able to fully concentrate on the details of his presentation and his mind would jump around uncontrollably.

Stress relief with EFT on his home situation created a space to work with his performance anxiety successfully, and he was able to give a confident and competent presentation.

One of the wonderful things about EFT is that it is quite literally in our own hands. We don't have to wait for a therapist to arrive to treat ourselves as and when necessary. Many, many people report preparing for their performance with EFT very successfully but also being immensely grateful that "they could go and tap in the toilet for a few rounds" to keep their stress levels down in the run up to the performance.

Using the Heart Healing and focusing on stress relief and improving the flow of energy at any time has also been very successful to keep a level head and personal power high "in the field."

Performance Trauma

The memory of past failed performances can often be significant blockages in the energy system and in the context of building up to the perfect performance state, there is every merit in treating those.

Use the EFT Story Protocol to tell the story of a performance trauma and tap through it, starting from the very beginning, step by step, until the entire story runs clear.

Please note: Always tap at least one round of EFT for "stress" before you start to tell the story of the performance trauma. As soon as you think in that direction, your energy system will become automatically stressed and de-stabilised. You need to be reasonably calm so you can tell a simple, cohesive story of the events that will contain the right set ups to tap on.

For example, Sahid had the following story, which started with the words, "When I was at school ..."

He noticed that even that caused him to feel more stressed, so he tapped on, "School," first of all. He said that throughout the round, he felt "all sorts of things, and all this stuff going through my mind and my body, there was a lot going on there!"

He started the story again, "When I was at school, I was really shy. Really shy. I couldn't look people in the eye ..."

This became the next set up, "I couldn't look people in the eye," with "eyes" as the set up phrase.

After this round he said, "That's such a problem, the audience looking at me, I still hate it when people are staring at me!"

He tapped on, "people staring at me," with the reminder phrase of, "staring." He felt he wanted to tap another round on the same set up, but in the middle of the round changed it to, "My father staring at me."

This caused a big energy release and he felt he wanted to move on with the story.

"When I was at school, I was very shy. I couldn't look people in the eye. This teacher made me come up in front to read out a poem I had written. I thought I would die!"

At first, Sahid thought he wanted to tap on "I thought I would die," but then changed his mind and said, "I want to tap on that teacher. He was cruel. He knew how afraid I was and he enjoyed it, enjoyed making me suffer!"

The set up was, "cruel teacher," with the reminder phrase of cruel teacher. This also caused a big energy release - our code word for spontaneous crying.

After this round, Sahid looked thoughtful and said, "I don't really feel anything now about the wanting to die any more. It's like that wasn't important, it was about the cruel teacher. I felt so abandoned, so alone."

He tapped on "abandoned and alone," with "alone" as the reminder phrase. After that, he took a deep breath and started to smile. "It's ok to be alone when you're up front," he said, smiling. "It's lonely at the top!" and there, he actually started to laugh.

Afterwards, Sahid said, "That was so funny, when I thought, it's lonely at the top something happened, I can't describe it, like something clicked together for me. I am always aiming for the top, and being up front, that's the leadership position, that's where you tell people what to do - my rightful place, in fact!"

He felt empowered and excited at the challenge and opportunity of performance in his field, and later reported that this EFT treatment had been a complete turning point for him, both personally as well as professionally.

We cannot promise that in EFT self help, you'll get a major breakthrough as Sahid did as quickly as this; but that doesn't matter. Simply keep on tapping step by step through your own performance traumas, one at a time, and don't stop until you have really had an energy experience that was a real personal breakthrough for you.

It isn't so important that you should get it all right on the first pass; you've got days, weeks, months to figure out for yourself how your performance problems "work," what caused them, and how it all hangs together for you.

If in doubt, simply focus on "stress" and tap for that - this will always improve your performance, make your body stronger, make you think smarter, and help you feel better inside.

Performance Enhancement

"Everything you can do, you can do better - with EFT!"

It is an absolute fact that there isn't a single thing we can't improve upon by improving the flow of energy through our energy bodies. With maximum energy flow, we can really enter those mystical Zen states of enhanced performance that seems supernatural to those who don't understand the very real effects of energy on everything we do, think, and feel.

People tend to think of performance enhancement as just "fixing what is broken," and EFT can do that, absolutely.

Whatever your shortcomings in performance, simply make a list of them and tap through them in your own time, until the blocks have been removed.

You can tap on global performance issues such as, "I'm tone deaf and I can't sing!" to create a breakthrough to being able to access your natural and God given talents at last.

You can also tap on extremely specific performance issues, such as "I feel slightly out of control when potting long balls with a rest," or, "The 9 iron is my least favourite golf club," for example.

However, the best and most exciting type of performance enhancement is to tap EFT on something you are already very good at.

We have found time and time again in the practice of EFT that when you raise performance in an area a person is already very good at, their general performance lifts across the board - they are all of a sudden to *also* do things better that were previously troublesome.

It is possible that when we access high energy flow states and improve them even further, smaller and other energy blockages get simply washed away in the process; regardless, tapping on your best aspects is very motivational, fun to do and might open up whole new realms of endeavour, allowing you to go "where no man has gone before," quite literally.

This is very exciting and the unique feature of modern energy work, which brings us to this consideration on performance.

The Joy Of Performance

There is nothing as deeply satisfying, en-joy-able, motivational and inspiring than doing something beautifully - doing something better than just well.

In many ways, the experience of performing beyond what you thought you ever could is life changing. It changes your self concept as a bye-the-bye; it really energizes your life and makes you very keen to do it again, to do more of it, to do it even better and to discover where your real limits might lie.

And time, and time again, we have found that what we thought were our limits were no such thing, they were just walls, blockages beyond which we could not go before because we didn't know how.

In truth, performance without joy is always a wasted opportunity for everyone involved, and not just the performer.

Whatever performances are required of us, whenever, with whom or where, we now have another target for our performances - namely that we, the performers, should experience the pure joy of performance as we do it.

Imagine a world in which all people performed their performances - as lovers, as doctors, as public speakers, as sports people, as cooks, as parents, as therapists, as mechanics, as entertainers - with that joy of performance shining from them, lifting them, imbuing all they do with power, with energy and with love.

That's a wonderful thought, and something we can keep there, to aim for, to use as a goal and target for our own performances and keep striving for that joy of performance - accept no substitutes!

EFT & Play

It is beginning to be rediscovered what superior form of human endeavour "playing" really is.

When we consider a young child at play, we can notice how deeply immersed they are in their activities; how learning is taking place as the child interacts with their environment; mind, body and spirit all together in the same place at the same time, in perfect harmony.

The experience of real play is very attractive; people prefer to play, rather than to work. Of course we also have all this societal entrainment that play has to stop and has to be replaced by "hard work" in order to achieve something; yet any person who loves their work will describe the experience of work to be the same as a child would play.

In the practice of modern energy work and EFT it was discovered that something interesting happens when we start to clear out blockages and improve the energy flow. You do this enough and work begins to turn to play in the experience of a person.

A young businessman who had started to use EFT for stress in his start up company said, "Once I started tapping, I could feel that original sense of excitement about my company coming back, that joy of building something that belongs to you, with your own hands, to be the master of your destiny and it's up to you how good it's going to be. It lifted me, gave me so much more energy but also I was much clearer on what had to be done.

"I am going to work these days with the excitement of a kid on Christmas morning, only better. Being in business is so much fun!"

Positive excitement, the sense of having fun and really enjoying oneself, using one's faculties of mind, body and spirit to their best advantage is the very definition of play. It is also the very definition of having good, positive energy flow in the energy body; so the old adage of, "Whatever you have to do, make a game of it!" can be made quite real with EFT.

Conversely, when something seems to be hard work, or has become hard work, painful and difficult, stressful and best avoided, we can simply say that this is an effect of energy blockages, and if we apply EFT, the most unlikely forms of human endeavour turn from hard work into fun.

Here is an example. This lady, Ellen, loved her job but hated doing her taxes or any form of book keeping. This led to her business running into big trouble, causing more and more stress, the longer it went on; and now was getting into dangerous territory where large fines and potentially even prison sentences started to loom on the horizon.

She went to see an EFT practitioner for stress at work; the practitioner soon identified the problem with the book keeping, which was tracked back to having had bad experiences in a maths class when Ellen was at school.

This was treated with numerous rounds of EFT, until Ellen cried out that the previously confusing and painful symbols on the blackboard she remembered all of a sudden turned into legible, simple numbers and equations; the Healing Event had happened and she felt happy and excited about numbers and maths for the first time in her life.

"What was so amazing," said Ellen, "Was that I just fell in love with the numbers! All of a sudden, it was so clear to me - they're just there to help, to help you organise your reality, to make things simple and easy. Numbers are great, they are fun, and I could never see that before!"

She went home and started to organise her bookwork and some months later, during a check back from her practitioner, reported that that sense of "fun" and "playing" had stayed with her and her books were perfectly organised now. Plus, her income had doubled as well as she now "experienced a tremendous sense of satisfaction to see the numbers work, and the turnover grow!"

What this case demonstrates is that it is our experience of a thing, not the thing in and of itself, is what makes the difference between work, and play. When we are having good experiences with something, be this maths, mountain climbing, digging in the garden, cataloguing a library, building a brick wall, writing a novel, creating a database or chiselling a monumental sculpture from granite, we are playing. When our experience of something is negative or painful, it becomes hard work.

Ellen "hated" numbers and all that related to them; they were physically painful to her, caused her stress and this destroyed her natural abilities to handle numbers with ease and enjoy the benefits of well organised systems with numerical representations. With the pain and stress replaced by joy, happiness and excitement, she had fun with numbers, much in the same way as any high class mathematician in love with numbers would experience when they go to "work."

We can learn two important things from this.

The first is to broaden our horizons and expectations of what fun can be, what play is, and how much and how often we can personally get to play.

In essence, *everything is open to become play* - we simply need to remove our blockages to these endeavours and have good experiences with them, to replace the old bad experiences which caused the blockages in the first place.

We can make a list of our own personal "hard work" challenges - all of which can be turned by definition into a real experience of "play" by the application of EFT.

If you are now wondering if such tasks as taking the trash out or cleaning the toilet could ever be "made into a game," by all means, try it out for yourself. It is simply extraordinary how the whole world changes when energy flow improves, and improves more until a threshold shift is reached and it is a great EFT learning experience, so do be playful and test it for yourself.

This ability to turn hard work into play by improving energy flow through our energy body has another repercussion, and this is to question whether we can do certain things that we thought we couldn't do at all.

If you think about it for a moment, what kind of things do you think and feel you could never possibly do, ever?

For example, some people feel they could never run a marathon. It is a complete mystery how anyone could do that, and inconceivable that someone could do that *and enjoy themselves* doing it!

Or how about writing a 500,000 word novel? Or spending a month writing a computer program? The people who do those things *love* doing that, they would rather do that than anything else in the world, and structurally, they are just the same as any one of us.

Pick something that you personally feel you could never possibly do and never mind enjoy doing, and tap a few rounds of EFT on it. Notice how your conception of the whole topic changes, how your feelings towards the activities change and you start to think and feel differently about this.

This is extraordinary and opens the doors to be able to do new things, try new things, and have brand new experiences in areas that were previously thought to be completely out of bounds for a person. Over time, it leads to a real re-assessment of the self concept as we begin to learn that we may have had painful experiences in the past and because of those, gave up on areas of human endeavour as "not being for me in this life."

The practice of EFT has shown time and time again that just about everything can be "for me in this life" - and it can be thoroughly enjoyed, in that whole hearted, mind/body/spirit all in the same place, at the same time way that defines true "play."

Finally, there is the matter of taking that which is already good and making it even better still. Turning hard work into play is wonderful; but tapping a few rounds of EFT on your favourite play activity is extraordinary. We firmly believe that the limits of what a human being can achieve when they get their own blocks out of the way have absolutely not been reached, not by a long shot.

There is always room for loving that which we already love to do even more; of enjoying it even more; of using this to energize and inspire us even more.

It may well be that those mysterious Zen states of perfect alignment, perfect performance and perfect happiness are indeed, play at its best - and with EFT and given a bit of time, we can definitely evolve all our activities in that direction.

EFT & Self Esteem

It is an extraordinary observation that self esteem and energy flow are so directly correlated to one another, they are to all intents and purposes, one and the same.

Stressed people will naturally think and say negative things about themselves, and the more stressed they are, the more negative it all becomes.

Emotions likewise become more and more painfully negative, the more energy flow is blocked and disturbed; and when stress gets high enough, we move from self doubt via real negativity to actual self loathing and self hatred, which can cumulate in self mutilation and suicide.

- **We have found time and time again that as soon as you improve the flow of energy through the energy body, people's self esteem rises in direct proportion.**

A person who started out their EFT treatments with the set up of, "I'm a total idiot and I hate myself!" goes through the stages of, "Well, perhaps I'm not a total idiot all the time ..." as the worst stress is released, then as energy flow improves towards the Zero point, "I've done some pretty stupid things in my time, but I guess that doesn't make me an idiot ..." moving on towards, "I can be quite smart, I should give myself more credit," as we're getting into the + side of the SUE scale and cumulating in, "I'm an intelligent, powerful and capable human being!" when energy flow is high, +8 and above.

This happens so globally and so reliably with people who use EFT Energy that we have come to the conclusion that the very presence of low self esteem or negative thinking/feeling about the self simply denotes that a person is stressed. With this observation, we can stop asking questions such as, "What's wrong with me that I hate myself so much?" and answering them with a never ending list of terrible things that have happened in our lives; instead, when we start feeling negativity, it is simply a sign that we're stressed and the answer to "What's wrong with me?!" is, "You are stressed!" every time.

We can also ask some new questions, and this is the beginning of a new relationship with ourselves and a different take on self esteem altogether.

216

We can ask, "What is causing the most stress in my life, right now?" to get to the real problems in the energy system.

Modern energy work is not psychology. It is very structural and deals with real injuries and blockages in the energy system. As such, it is immaterial where they came from, we simply treat them and then we feel better.

If you have ever or still currently feel you suffer from "low self esteem," take heart. You are only suffering from energy body stress which produces negative thoughts (and not just about you, about everything!) as a natural side effect.

Find out what stresses you most in your life, right now. Make a list and treat these set ups with EFT until you don't just feel better, but fully energized. Then you will feel very differently, and you won't be thinking or feeling negatively about yourself any longer.

Understanding that negative feelings about the self are always "only" energy body stress indicators also changes the way you think about other people. If you pay attention, you will be able to discern that direct correlation between stress and expressions of "low self esteem" in friends, family, in the media all around us.

It also gives you the direct path if you wish to improve someone else's self esteem - de-stress them, re-energize them by all and any means, including using Proxy EFT to assist their better energy flow, and "a more positive self concept" will be the direct result.

Finally, our understanding of modern energy work also teaches us that "self esteem" isn't something that a person does, or does not have. The level of positivity or negativity at any given moment is directly dependent on the flow of energy through the energy body and it can therefore change like the weather, depending on what's happening inside and outside of a person.

We don't need to make a special effort to work on our self esteem; if we simply pay attention to energy body stress in general and do what we can to keep our energy levels at least reasonably positively high, good self esteem follows as surely as day follows night.

We can also understand and allow for the moments when the energy system went down and the corresponding negative thoughts and emotions occurred; and we can learn from this what triggers us, who and what has beneficial effects on our energy flow, and who and what causes us energy body stress. This is simple, global and holistic; and it also means that we can have more self esteem any time we need, a round or two of EFT will do the trick.

EFT & Relationships

Before the onset of modern energy work, dealing with the intense emotions of relationships was fraught with difficulty and often not just unsuccessful but even counter productive.

When we keep energy in mind, improving relationships, repairing relationships and even the ubiquitous "cutting the ties that bind us" becomes logical and perfectly doable with EFT.

If this wasn't enough reason to celebrate, with Proxy EFT we also have a way to not just change ourselves, but to change others as well. This puts an end to the idea that the only way relationships can be changed is by changing oneself and that one has no power over other people; how this could ever have been held to be true is a mystery to us.

The principle of improving relationships with EFT could not be simpler:

- **Remove the blockages that stand in the way of a a free flowing energy exchange.**

This is not only the golden rule for love based relationships; it is also the same rule for relationships which are no longer wanted or needed in order to let them simply flow away.

In essence, there is only one way to have successful relationships across the board with anything, not just people, and that is to have a free flowing, powerful energy system that was literally born to relate with all the world in a healthy and energizing fashion.

A global question we can therefore ask is:

"What gets in my way to have a healthy relationship with X?"

X could be anything - a lover, a mate, a friend, a child, a companion animal. It can also be an artefact (*see EFT & Artefacts*), a country, a football club, an addictive substance, a company, an entity or a concept.

The global rules for healthy relationships apply to every one and every thing; and they are simply that blockages are bad and more energy flow is good.

There are no exceptions to this rule, even though we may "feel" that there are some Xs we could never have a healthy relationship with. We feel that way because of an energy blockage, and the more severe that energy blockage is, the more we will of course "feel bad" when we consider our particular Xs.

In that way, the global rule for all healthy relationships can be reversed and used as a diagnostic, to tell us where our worst energy blockages are situated in our energy body.

We can ask, "What X could I never have a healthy relationship with?"

Make a list of those Xs and tap through the list, one X at a time.

The very first X you treat with EFT in that way will demonstrate to you how "emotional freedom" actually really works, and how wonderful it feels, how empowering, when you get free of an unwanted X and your energetic entanglements with it.

The more we reject any relationship, the more important it is that we should treat ourselves for this; and the greater the benefits we receive as major energy blockages are taken out and healthy energy flow returns to systems which may have been lying fallow for decades.

Here is an example of an extreme X and what happened when a person took that on to treat their relationship with EFT.

David, a middle aged gentleman, had been sexually abused during his stay in a religious boarding school by one particular teacher as a young boy. For the next 5 decades which followed, he suffered from a huge variety of symptoms and major emotional disturbances which led him to attempt to commit suicide repeatedly. For all those years he also suffered from nightmares in which his abuser featured prominently.

David said, "My relationship with that man has dominated my life, has ruined my life. As much as I've tried to forget, for all I've ever tried to do to block him out, he is always with me, whatever I do, wherever I go. I can't get away from him."

Recurring nightmares are always a message from the energy mind, which is trying to tell us in its own metaphorical language that there is a major problem in the energy system, so that we wake up and do something about it.

Not knowing that we even had energy systems, these calls remained unanswered and became more and more disturbed and disturbing over time.

When we use EFT to work on a relationship and improve the flow of energy to the point where we reach emotional freedom, we literally "fix that problem" at last and then the nightmares will stop.

David started his self help EFT simply tapping on the stress he experienced when "he thought in that man's direction."

It took him a couple of weeks until he felt ready to tap "on that man."

He used the set up phrase and reminder phrase of, "That man," throughout many rounds, and many of these were extremely emotional.

However, as David said, "I've been an emotional wreck all my life. The crying I did throughout the EFT treatments felt different, more like a proper release and not so much like it used to be, when I was just wailing."

At one point in the treatment, David had the experience that all of a sudden, "that man," who had been "right in his face" all along, started to move backwards and seemed to fade away. David got scared when that happened, but realised this right away and tapped on "I'm scared." After that round he said, "I could feel that man going away at last but when I felt that I thought, what am I going to do now? I don't know how to live without that, without him."

This is also a normal and natural reaction; what David described as the man "moving away" was a major re-organisation in his energy system which had been stuck in that state ever since he had been 9 years old.

David changed the set up after the first round of "I'm scared," to "I'm confused." After that round, he sighed deeply and said that he felt a sense of immense peace and clarity, as though he could see his whole life for the first time from an adult perspective.

There were other things David tapped for over the course of the next weeks, including the loss of life, the 50 years he would never get back now, but as is the case, he reported that, "I appreciate my life so much more now, I've learned so much, and for the first time it feels as though there actually will be a sunrise tomorrow, a new day, a new day for me."

This is a high end example of treating a serious relationship with EFT; David gave his permission for this to be told to encourage others to face their "personal demons" and evolve their relationships beyond what was there before. David said, "I encourage anyone who has something like my 'that man' in their lives, overshadowing their lives all the time, to have a go and tap on it. If you're afraid, that's ok, tap on the fear first. Learn to trust EFT and that it works for you first. Take your time but keep tapping. To get free and clear of that man, I can't even describe how I feel about that, or how grateful I am."

Relationships are strands of connections through which energy flows. When these channels of communications flow clearly, relationship problems of all kinds can be resolved; and existing loving relationships can be made more deep, more profound and transform into whole new experiences of how much love we can give and receive.

People feel unloved when there is no energy coming in; and this might not be because there is a lack of love energy, but because they can't process it correctly.

A simple example of this is when a person's heart was broken and now they can't fall in love as once they did.

Another person comes along and offers all the love they have to give, but as long as the heart remains broken (a metaphorical description for a real existing energy blockage in the heart), it cannot be received properly.

We can tap EFT on the broken heart and transform not just this one relationship, but all the relationships the formerly broken hearted person has, and not just with lovers.

There is a lot of love in the world, from friends and relatives, of course; from pets, from nature, from God itself who made the amazing world with all the energies it has to offer us. All of that is energy, all of that is love and it is all and everywhere, all the time.

In many ways, it is up to us to clear our energy blockages so we can (finally) receive all that love that is on offer and freely available to us all.

This is also a good place to start when we want to improve any of our relationships with anyone at all - with ourselves, and with finding what stands in the way of having wonderful experiences of giving and receiving energy and love today.

This can be past traumas of love, rejections, unrequited love; often, it is an absence of love experienced, or not having received the kind of love that was needed at a crucial time in our lives.

The beautiful thing about treating ourselves for our love blockages is that all we have to do is make a list, tap through it, make sure we get our energy flow high to the positive end of the SUE scale and the world of love is our oyster.

As we learn to help ourselves, so our understanding of the energy processes of love and relationships grows. We understand how stress influences the ability to give and receive love; we can clear our old blockages to love and activate our own love systems more.

That naturally leads to becoming far more compassionate and far less judgemental about our fellow human beings in turn; this now relieves even more stress, and so an upward lifting love spiral is born, where energies are exchanged easily and readily, and we literally learn to lift each other higher, and higher.

Finally, we can use EFT to keep our relationships flowing nicely no matter what life throws at us. Especially in long standing and intimate relationships, such as we would find amongst lovers, mates and parents with their children, siblings and families, business partners - every day bits of energetic garbage can build up and block up the energy system.

Becoming aware of when such things happen, and treating them immediately with EFT, is such a wonderful thing. We have all heard stories of feuds in families that last a lifetime over "that potato salad incident in

1949" - what a waste of opportunities to learn, relate, love and support one another!

Keeping loving relationships garbage free is the most amazing gift of modern energy work, an ongoing journey of discovery of what real human relationships can be like, and a very powerful source of energetic support across our times of life.

In conclusion, EFT gives us a tool to really address our relationship problems in a whole new way. We can use it to heal our own blockages and disturbances in relationships with people who are alive as well as those who have already passed on.

We can improve the way we give and receive love on every level, and look forward to having brand new experiences of relationships which no human being has ever experienced before - and that is certainly achievable, and a wonderful thought.

EFT & Sex

There are no more powerful flows in the human energy system than those related to sex and procreation; and there is no topic for modern human beings that is more blocked, convoluted and generally mismanaged than is the sexual energy circuitry.

We have talked much about energy body stress and how it affects everything we do; and it is a simple fact that at least 75% of this stress is located in the sexual circuitry, whether people like this, or not.

A very wise teacher once remarked that people come to him with all these problems - from insomnia to low energy, from depression to anger, from not having enough money to not finding enough self respect, and if they simply treated their sexual problems, most of that would simply disappear, for it is only a symptom.

What so powerfully exacerbates the problems in the sexual circuitry of every man, woman and child walking around today is the enormous amount of denial.

People simply do not realise that they are supposed to be powerful sexual beings; that this is a part of their structure no-one can escape from; that this doesn't go away with age, because the energy system isn't age bound like the body and doesn't rely on such things as hormones or physical circumstances; that their sexual circuitry is all important for every level of function, endeavour, self belief, self healing, creativity, power in mind, body and spirit - and that this applies to you, as well!

The sexual circuitry is always there, it is always active even when it has been relegated to dark corners, here and there alone; and if we can start to think more systemically, less judgementally and more healthily about our sexual energy flows, we can gain traction in personal development that was previously absent.

The Fear Of Sex

The first thing we need to hold on to is that working with energy body and removing damaging blockages and injuries so energy flow improves has nothing to do with the physical act of going out and actually having sex.

That is completely under your control - if the energy flows are working correctly and you are in full possession of mind, body and spirit and all their various faculties.

We need to also make that distinction between taking good care of the energy body and essentially rescuing it from a lifetime of torture and all those practical warnings about having physical sex and the bad repercussions this can have.

This sub chapter is entitled, "The fear of sex," but we can simply think in terms of sexual blocks, injuries and reversals that we would be much better off without, in every way imaginable.

Simply tap a round of mindful EFT for "Sex." If this thought frightens or disturbs you, or if you honestly believe that "this has NOTHING to do with ME!" (!!) then tap a round or two for "Stress" first, and then take that scary plunge and tap on "Sex."

Pay attention to what happens in your body as you slowly and mindfully tap each point, remaining focused on sexual energy flows in your body and with a will to have those be nothing other than *healthy*.

You might find that all manner of reversals become revealed in the process.

There are so many different ways in which people literally "reverse away" from the subject -

- *I'm too old, this doesn't concern me.*

In the contrary! The older you are, the more your physical body desperately needs high flow in the energy system to keep it working as well and for as long as it possibly can. Remember this is NOT about physical sex, it's only about energy.

- *My sex life is just fine, I don't need this.*

This is great, and congratulations, but once again, this is not about physical sex, it's only about energy flows. Do the exercise!

- *I'm terrified I might want to have sex, or more sex, or start to really crave physical sex and become a sex monster!*

When mind, body and spirit are working properly together, we are not fear riddled, we are not driven by our emotions or feelings, and we never think such crazy thoughts. You are just stressed. Please, take a moment to de-stress with EFT, and then de-stress some more. A mature, adult, capable human being is in charge of what they do and when they do it - as you will be, with all that fear and terror and stress out of the way.

- *I have a myriad of problems, and none of them have to do with sex. I'm going to skip this chapter now and read the others instead.*

Please don't. Do remember how powerful and all pervasive the sexual circuitry really is. When that's blocked and broken, people don't stand a chance to live powerful, delightful, creative and satisfying lives. That's a simple "fact of life."

- *I've had terrible experiences of a sexual nature and I am too afraid to start tapping for sex on my own.*

If this is the case, you should certainly make contact with a professional EFT practitioner and get some movement going in that way. You can request "Secret Therapy" so you don't have to talk about anything at all, and you can tap on, "That problem of mine," with full support from the EFT practitioner. Again, if you do know you really need to start addressing this so important topic (finally) then please use EFT to just help you to get ready to start on the topic in the first place.

Make a list of all that you're afraid of and tap through it, gently and lovingly, one step at a time. You've already been hurt enough, we only want to make it better, get some help to those places in your energy system where the pain still resides today, so you can lead a better life. Please be gentle with yourself, but also please continue to move towards healing at a pace that is right for.

EFT & Sex Abuse Survivors

The reason that the symptoms in sex abuse and especially, child sex abuse survivors are so tremendous and far reaching is exactly because the sexual circuitry is so important in the human energy body.

Indeed, it is the suffering of sex abuse survivors which can really demonstrate to us how powerful a system that is, and how it affects absolutely everything a person may try to do in their life - across all topics of endeavour, across the totality of mind, body and spirit.

There are further, many more people who are in fact, sex abuse survivors, and don't know this, don't realise it, because their sexual traumas took place inside a "loving relationship," or a marriage, or were deemed to be a normal right of passage, or something that "just happens" to young people, to people in our society.

There was, for example, a lady who had been forced to have sex against her will for 20 years, day in, day out, come rain or shine, no matter what her physical, emotional or mental condition at the time. She had all the symptoms of a sex abuse survivor but never thought of that as a potential cause for her many problems - physical, emotional and mental! - as she really believed this treatment was a normal part of being married.

Another lady had been forced into sexual activities against her will by her first boyfriend, treated roughly and without consideration and likewise, never suspected her symptoms, which were those of a sex abuse victim, had anything to do with the deep trauma of her first sexual experiences. She believed that what had happened to her was "normal and natural, it's like that for anyone when they first start out."

A young man who had been used as a sex toy by an older woman and then discarded likewise thought what had happened to him was normal and natural. Indeed, he felt he should count himself lucky to have received this treatment and never suspected that many of his physical, mental and emotional problems stemmed from what was absolutely also sexual abuse at a vulnerable, fragile time.

The really important thing to focus on when dealing with all sex abuse survivors is what the condition of the energy system is like right here, right now.

The first thing to address as always is energy body stress.

Sex abuse survivors have their most important energy channels in total disarray; their energy flows had to re-route around the problem ereas, causing very strange and unusual emotions, thoughts, behaviours that make no sense if we don't take the energy system into consideration.

When we do, it becomes clear what has happened, why this has happened, the effects it had and also, what we need to do to evolve beyond this and restore better flow to the energy body.

As a result of this re-wiring around the problem ereas, sex abuse survivors experience much, much higher levels of global stress than average, and this stress exists all the time.

It doesn't stop when such a person is put into a nice, peaceful environment as this stress is linked to the complicated re-routings in the energy system.

This makes the energy system fragile and unstable; it tries to do its work as best it can but is severely hampered and can't take high levels of stress.

This is systemic, has nothing to do with will power or character, and it needs to be addressed urgently by applying stress relief and improving energy flow *all the time*.

There are lots of opportunities to work with stress release for sex abuse survivors.

Almost everything that seems straightforward and easy for "normal" people causes stress and anxiety - from crossing the road, to going shopping, from calling someone on the phone to writing an email, even going to bed and getting up again in the morning can be an absolute ordeal as the the already stressed system constantly teeters on the edge of cataclysm.

To survive at all, people who suffer from this have had to train themselves to ignore impossibly high level stress and try to function somehow anyway. They will use whatever they can to help them in this endeavour; and again, this goes across the board from using food, behavioural patterns, any form of medication, any action, any person and any "thing" that can help in the endless struggle with everything, all the time.

It can be very scary for sex abuse survivors to even start to tune in on their stress levels, as this is the opposite direction of attention to what they've been trying to do for a long time, decades in some cases. Yet, to start on that all important journey to get the energy system to function in a healthier, more powerful way, this is exactly what has to be done.

Long before we start to apply EFT to the causative sexual traumas, we need to de-stress when an opportunity presents itself.

It is a good idea to make a list of "stress spikes" and treat these first of all.

For example, Lucy had a terrible time getting ready to go out and leave her flat.

From the very thought of having to go out, stress levels would rise and rise and eventually "cumulate in some total insanity involving make up, clothes and crying and throwing myself about like a total lunatic on occasions."

Lucy started to use EFT simply on going out at first. As soon as she knew she had to go out somewhere, and long before that time ever arrived, she would self treat with EFT, using the set up phrase of "Going out." This would calm her down and she would forget about having to go out tomorrow for a little while, then think of it again and the stress would come back. But she simply tapped on it again and reported that it really helped and the stress wasn't building up as much any longer.

On her first try, she managed to get out of her flat, dressed reasonably appropriately for the occasion, and there had been no "meltdown," for which she was very grateful.

Lucy said, "It was like there was hope again. I was still - I don't know, terrified, crazy about the whole going out thing, getting dressed and all of that, but I wasn't so out of control any more.

"I could feel the EFT was really doing something, really helping me. I've never felt anything could do that apart from drugs, but the EFT felt better, much better."

Working on daily stress challenges like this also does something else that is very important, especially for abuse survivors.

It gives the person time to practice EFT, to get to know it and how their own energy body responds to it. It gives a person experience in the use of EFT and also develops trust in the fact that EFT really can help release emotions and stuck energies and make us feel much better.

This is an important learning process *before* we go to discuss specifics of the sexual traumas and memories relating to the core problems in the energy system.

It is also very important that at least some stress has been alleviated before we get "there," to quite literally empower the person and have them be much clearer of mind. This helps with recall and also is the source of the courage we need when we get ready to address serious problems, blockages and injuries.

Making stress relief with EFT the first goal and focusing on that first of all is the foundation for sex abuse survivors, and this is certainly doable in self help. The aim is to get ready to be able to engage an EFT practitioner so that the person is not alone when it comes to facing the deep problems and the worst of the old injuries.

There are many people in our societies who need help with their serious problems but are too stressed to seek help - or we could simply say, they are not ready, in a very structural way.

It is hoped that some who read this will take it upon themselves to work with their own stress, one step at a time, until they feel ready, willing and able to move into the treatment phase for the deep injuries in the energy system. When it is done correctly, working with EFT step by step to release stress and re-empower the energy system, the path into healing even extreme sex abuse trauma need never be painful or hard.

Every stress relieved from the energy system makes it stronger and more powerful; and in a treatment program that focuses always on stress relief and empowering the energy system slowly, more and more as time goes on, we get to a place when a person is really ready to take the final steps and deal with the core problems directly.

This is ecological, the right way to proceed and each person gets to have their own individual journey, in their own time and no sooner than they are ready, willing and able to take the next step.

Improving Your Sex Life & EFT

We have spoken much about the energy of sex; but we can certainly improve our physical experience with sex as well, having better orgasms and in general, improving our sex life with EFT in a very practical way.

Answer this simple question, "What stands in the way of me having much better/even better sex experiences?" As before, make a list of the answers - and simply tap EFT through the list, a session for each list item at a time. Putting more energy into one's sex life can really transform the experience of having sex in physicality, so don't be shy - and if you're shy, try some EFT on the topic.

In conclusion, there may be merit in writing out "EFT & SEX!" on a piece of paper and placing it into your treatment bowl so you can be reminded every so often. For many people, sexual repression and sexual denial is such a practised thing that the thought just drops away, time and time again, and nothing is ever done to improve, heal, repair and empower the sexual circuitry.

As the wise teacher said, whatever the problem, try tapping on sex. With those powerful energies flowing smoothly, many problems lessen and are much simpler to solve; and there are some problems which will never be solved unless some attention is (finally!) given to the sexual circuitry.

EFT & Spirituality

It is interesting to observe that modern, energy based EFT is a form of spirituality; after all, we are treating the spirit dimension in the mind, body, *spirit* triad when we apply EFT to our problems.

Many people tap EFT every day; few would consider it a spiritual practice and many don't even know how or why EFT manages to effectively release negative emotions and make us feel better.

However, for those are so inclined, EFT can practically transform the experience of religion and all spiritual practices, simply by removing what stands in the way to the full expression and sensation of a living spirituality in action.

By way of a simple example, one can use EFT to deepen one's understanding of scripture, regardless to which religious persuasion this belongs. EFT can help with "doubt" - doubt, after all, is only a form of energy body stress, and if we treat it with EFT and improve the energy flow to the high + side of the SUE scale, doubt melts away and is replaced by empowering certainty.

It is important to re-iterate at this point that you cannot tap reality away with EFT, nor use EFT to deepen illusion.

Real reality rules supreme and when we "clear the doors of perception" with EFT, we always get closer to reality, and this also includes the reality of spiritual experience in human beings.

There are many different ways in which EFT can be used to enhance the practices of spirituality. Whether it is using EFT to help us formulate more perfect and heart felt prayers, meditations and devotions; or to have a more powerful personal relationship with saints, prophets, symbols or concepts; to deal successfully with spiritual trauma and negative experiences; or simply to explore on a personal level, as we say, "Everything can work better with EFT!"

We should also not underestimate the quite extraordinary effects simple stress relief has on all spiritual practices, and how naturally people become more and more expansive and spiritual in their thoughts and feelings when energy flow moves towards the +10, the optimal energy flow.

In these high positive energy states (which are only our birthright, nothing special, unusual or superhuman, this is how we are supposed to *be* all the time!) we do feel connected to the world, to each other, to the Universe and often have a sense of a "living God," a creative order in action that is much more than just an abstract concept.

Each Healing Event is a form of enlightenment experience in the true sense of the word; our energy system literally lights up, starts to work better, and we understand more, feel completely different and new positive emotions and the world changes altogether in an instance.

With the very concept of the Healing Events, we even have a personal pathway of enlightenment laid out for us, if we wish to step upon it.

We can start by evolving the major events in our lives, good and bad alike for these produce the most reliable Healing Events when they are treated all the way to the end.

Simply by treating our own most pressing problems with EFT, theoretically we will become more and more enlightened as time goes on, and as our energy systems evolve and start to flow ever more powerfully, ever more smoothly.

This also *has to* lead us eventually towards new experiences, and here too, we do not have to be so afraid any longer to engage fully with heart and soul - should we experience failure and heart break, we can use EFT to put us not only back to rights, but use these very experiences through the Healing Event to further our enlightenment journey.

EFT & Weight Loss

When EFT first arrived on the scene, of course the people who obsess about weight loss jumped on it with both feet and started tapping like crazy. And they did lose weight - for a while. When they stopped tapping, it started to come back and this left them very disappointed. EFT was no better than any old diet that works for a few weeks and then it stops working and the weight starts to pile on again ...

The reason these disappointing results were happening was that back then, it simply wasn't clearly understood that EFT doesn't "melt fat mysteriously somehow" but that it works on the energy body instead.

Today, with much greater energy awareness and experience, we can take a different approach to the ubiquitous "weight loss" and gain better, faster and more direct results.

What have we learned from the failure of the early weight loss EFTers to "keep the weight off?"

The first thing that was learned was that there is no one single magic set up which will "cure the reason for piling on the weight forever."

There are many reasons for this, and many contributing factors; indeed one could say that the early EFTers learned a lot about themselves and solved many problems as they tapped, just not the propensity to consume more calories than the body can reasonably burn off again through activity.

The second thing, and this is very important, was that as long as they kept tapping, the positive results would keep happening. It was only when they stopped tapping that the weight loss would reverse.

We have learned that the energy system needs attention every day. It is no different from brushing our teeth, or eating a healthy meal, or sleeping for 8 hours - these things don't stay done, you can't just do them once and expect them to last a lifetime.

- **The energy body needs feeding, care and attention <u>all the time</u>.**

We need to be much more conscious of daily energy body maintenance, which includes turning stress into proactive, positive energy states as and when it happens; which includes solving whatever energy problems exist (see also *EFT & Sex*, for example!); and which also includes taking care of new problems and emotional shocks as and when they arise, as soon as possible.

The Energy Of Food

A lecturer at the annual AMT conference observed that "when we eat an orange, produced by the orange tree, which has been sucking the living daylights out of sun, soil, water for a whole season and has put all this into the orange, our energy bodies eat a ball of light!"

We may be physically eating the orange which lands in our physical stomach, but at the same time, the energy body is also eating - the orange made of energy, that powerful "ball of light" which enters the systems and provides us with living energy, energy for life.

Especially people who have problems with eating and with weight have all manner of energetic contortions and reversals to "sucking the living daylights out of a carrot," or any kind of food, for that matter.

What a person thinks and feels strongly influences the energy system. It may be so that when a highly reversed individual who is terrified of putting on weight eats an orange, they might be eating the physical orange, but the "ball of light" can't get into the system at all. "Food intake" is blocked at the energy level, the energy of the food can't get in, and so the energy body remains constantly underfed, constantly hungry, and constantly clamouring for more food.

The energy body "clamours" through our 6th sense, the body sensations that have no physical origin, which is exactly what you find when a person feels desperately hungry when their stomach is already full.

Further, when the energy body gets stressed, it needs even more "light food" to try and restore itself; so the more stressed an individual becomes, the more hungry they feel, the more they eat - and still, the light is not coming in.

This can then lead to all sorts of further problems, from anger to depression, from withdrawal to attention seeking (read, energy seeking!) behaviour and more and more uncontrollable emotions as the energy body goes from clamouring for food to SCREAMING for food. More physical food can be shovelled in but as long as the energy intake is blocked, the energy body remains unfed and dying of starvation still.

The first step therefore in addressing all eating related problems is to discover the energetic blockages to incoming food energies and essentially, remove the fear of food.

The Fear Of Food

The fatter a person presents, the more we can be sure that they are structurally afraid of food, in a direct cause and effect relationship.

This comes from the simple equation of "Food makes me fat = not eating food makes me healthy (and lovable)."

We can perfectly understand how a person could come to that conclusion; but we can also perfectly understand how this global rejection of food causes absolute chaos in the energy system.

We can ask a fat person, "On the SUE scale, how much do you love food?"

At the very least, we will find a sequential incongruency - sometimes I love it to +10, and then I hate it to -10! - which is clearly going to be a source of ongoing major stress, as we have to eat each day and go through this incongruency, conflict, "inner war," "endless battle with food," every day, over and over again.

We can start the process of getting a healthy, sensible relationship with the wondrous, life giving food by simply tapping a round of Mindful EFT on, "Food," and paying attention how that feels in the body.

Keep tapping rounds of EFT, as many as it takes, to get a congruent reading on the SUE scale that is in the high positives.

Please note: If you read this and you are afraid that you will start running to the fridge because you love food too much now and will get even fatter, don't be. You are sure to have had experiences of loving someone or something deeply and profoundly, and NOT wanting to eat them because of that.

All we are doing here is to improve the energy flow through your energy body, to give it some much needed nourishment and to take out some very deep, global reversals and blockages to the free flow of energy in, through and out your systems, and this is foundational for anyone wanting long term health in its widest metaphorical meaning.

During the Mindful EFT tapping for "Food," undoubtedly you will have thought many things, and might have remembered others.

By all means, take a moment to write down what you have found out about your relationship with food; you can write out potential new set ups or directions you want to explore with EFT on pieces of paper and place them in your EFT treatment bowl.

What is important at this time is to make sure the energy flow stays strong in the presence of "food" - always tap a round of EFT before eating anything with that simple, global set up statement that gets mind, body and spirit ready to accept the food you are about to eat.

People have often wondered how it is that certain types can look at a cake and put on 10 pounds; and other types can eat and eat and never get beyond being as skinny as a greyhound. Factoring in the fact that we also have energy bodies might explain this conundrum; either way, food will have to practically and physically also pass in, through and out, and that starts with receiving it gracefully and in a positive frame of mind, body and spirit.

On the topic of the fear of food, we must also mention more specific "food terrors," such as, "Fat makes me fat!" - "Sugar destroys my life!" - "Bananas are bad for you!" - "Eating a steak will give me a heart attack!" - "I'll die young if I eat salt!" - "Preservatives will make me age prematurely!" - "I'll get cancer if I flavour my food with soy sauce!" and God alone knows what other types of terrors lurk in the grocery cupboard, constantly fuelled by media reports and old wife's tales, all of which cause nothing but horrendous reversals that create havoc in any attempt at a healthy relationship with food.

Becoming aware of these fears - which are nothing but energy blockages, and they don't protect us, or serve us in any way, ever - is a first step to tackling them with EFT, and until we start to realise that just about anything we can find to eat will help us, make us healthier and stronger, if we eat logically, sensibly and from a state of real love.

Special Relationships With Food

The next step in the treatment of weightloss in EFT is to consider the "special foods" - foods that have special meanings, foods that feature highly and are often turned to in a moment of need, or a moment of greed, as the case may be.

These foods, and it doesn't matter if they have any physical "nutritional value" at all, are likely to have an exception and can enter into the energy body as balls of energy.

The exceptions come about as a result of highly positive experiences in the past, the Guiding Stars. A really wonderful experience was had, an energetic experience to be sure, and this creates what is in effect an **energy active drug** we then take when we feel the need for that kind of energy.

For example, there was a very overweight lady who would eat pink marshmallows quite literally by the sack.

She obviously realised this was a problem; she even knew that it was related to a time when she was a child and her stepfather had bought her a bag of pink marshmallows; he had commented as she was eating it that it was the same colour pink as the dress she was wearing and that she looked nice in it.

What she didn't realise was that **she was using the pink marshmallow like a prescription medication for low energy states**; and as with all medications, over time and over abuse, a desensitisation had built up to it and it didn't work any longer as once it did.

When we keep energy in mind, we can not only free ourselves from such unfortunate entanglements; we can even choose to use ONE pink marshmallow if ever such an energy injection was really needed.

However, as we are feeding the energy body and not the physical body, there is no need for that.

The lady placed the bag of pink marshmallow that had become a wholesale large sack over time and by now on the kitchen table before her, and simply focused on the longing she felt and tapped Mindful EFT. She said, "It was very strange. The more I tapped, the more I became aware of the feelings the marshmallow represented - that feeling of all's well with the world, it's summer, I'm pretty and I'm loved.

"It was a wonderful feeling, and I was feeling it for the first time since that day all those years ago.

"The feeling is inside me, I can feel like that any time I want - I just have to remember that day and it's right there!

"I felt such love for the pink marshmallow, and I had to laugh at the size of the sack! How big would it eventually had to become before I finally got it that I already know how that feels, that person who feels like that - that's me!"

We can report that this lady hasn't eaten another pink marshmallow since that day, but still loves them with all her heart and smiles as she passes them by on her way through the supermarket.

Make a list of your own favourite or addictive food and drink items.

Make it with care and expand it over time, so you can learn which kind of comfort food you turn to in a moment of crisis, and how the crisis and the food are matched perfectly in each case.

For example, there was a gentleman who would eat nothing but chicken soup when he was a little under the weather because that carried the caring energy he got from his grandmother when he was a small child.

Another gentleman would normally drink beer, but would turn to malt whiskey when stress at work reached a particular stage; this was based on drinking malt whiskey in the office with his first boss during similarly stress based circumstances, and feeling the stress drain away, and being safe and comfortable, with someone who knew what he was doing, and all was well with the world.

All these are examples of how we try to match the energy of the intake to the problem at hand; everybody does this without even knowing they're doing it, only as people get fatter and try to not do this sort of thing any longer, they unknowingly set up a custom made system of energy body starvation that can run out of control, and into obesity unless something is done about it at the energy levels, where all of this is happening.

Eating With Energy In Mind

For healthy eating to occur, we have to eat preferably with mind, body and spirit all in the same place and at the same time - and it would be even better still if this place was in the now, rather than trying to evoke energies from old experiences that are long been and gone.

Once we have relieved much of the fear of eating in general, and the terror of eating specific kinds of food, as well as the deep emotional entanglements to special food items and ingredients, we are ready to sit down for a candle lit dinner with energy in mind.

In truth, eating with energy in mind starts a long time before we get there.

It starts in the shopping stage, when we choose the ingredients for our meals, or choose the meals we will be ordering or buying.

We can ask the question, "Is this good energy food? Is this what my energy body really needs today?" and begin to develop a sense of which foods really are something that would make the energy body happy, here and now.

What the energy body needs to be strong and happy changes on a daily basis as the world turns through the seasons and stress rises and recedes in our lives; and for good energy practice we want to ask this question every time afresh, and not presuppose that because yesterday, tomatoes were "just the job," they will still be today. We might find that our energy body wants something else instead; indeed, what we want to do is to establish a standing communication with our energy body, a conversation that can guide us to our own personal healthy eating over time.

If we can take out the distortions in this process - the fear of food on the one side, and the fatal attraction to past glory foods on the other - we can get to a much more flexible and reasonable reading as to what needs to be eating, one meal at a time.

It is a very important step stone on the path to long term healthy eating to become aware of our feelings about food, for these tell us our problems and also guide us in the right direction once those problems have been solved with EFT.

Once we have decided on what kind of food we might want to eat, there is the matter of preparation. Clearly, if we cook our own food or prepare our own sandwiches, we want to do so with love. All we do with the food should have a desire to energize our food even further, prepare it in such a way that it becomes a delight to mind, body and spirit alike, and it really doesn't matter if one uses the poorest of ingredients, when a meal is prepared with love, we really do have "Soul Food" on our plates.

Finally, there is the meal itself. If we follow the path of energy as well as pure nutrition, we want to eat mindfully, reverently even, treasuring each mouthful and paying attention how it makes us feel inside, physically, mentally and emotionally, all at the same time, in the same place.

For people with serious weight issues it is strongly recommended to take at least some meals in silence, without talking to someone else, without being distracted by radio or TV, without thinking about anything else than just the food on the plate, and the experience of consuming it.

This mindful eating can help us have wonderful eating experiences; it can also give the space for more or other fears, topics, ideas and reversals to emerge which we can then go on to treat with further rounds of EFT.

A final important tip on eating with energy in mind is to take it easy, and allow yourself the time you need to really resolve all the various problems around eating and food, one round of EFT at a time.

This is not a diet; it is learning a different way of living in a world that does not just consist of flesh and bone, calories and fat alone. It doesn't matter if there are set backs or falling back into old behaviour patterns under stress. If you keep energy in mind and keep tapping to make yourself and your energy body feel better, eventual success isn't just guaranteed, it becomes inevitable.

EFT & Exercise

Exercising more to lose weight and in general, leading a more energized life style is of course of the essence as well, and here too, EFT can really help if it is applied with energy in mind.

For a really holistic and correct approach to exercising mind, body and spirit we cannot go on to tread the treadmills whilst the mind, and therefore the energy system, is watching TV or is somewhere else altogether.

- **Real exercise happens when mind, body and spirit are all in the same place, at the same time.**

In the context of exercise for weight loss, we want to engage the energy body as much as possible - we want to engage in exercise that feels good emotionally, that feels exciting, delightful, soothing, or uplifting.

Dancing, swimming and walking in nature are natural activities that engage all of us, especially if we do so in a mindful way.

Of course, the more weight a person carries, the harder and more painful it becomes to exercise; this not motivational in the least, and can lead to a serious build up of exercise trauma over time.

A person may have tried to exercise but found it difficult and painful; so they gave up on it, thinking they were weak and doomed to get fatter. Every person with weight problems has that in their history somewhere; and here we can immediately find a great application for EFT, namely to help us overcome our fear of exercise, and to get a totally different understanding of what exercise is, and how you do it.

On the SUE scale, how painful do you expect exercise that would help you lose weight to be? The lower the number, the more pain you expect; and the less likely it is that you would put yourself through that any time soon.

Do a full round of Mindful EFT on the topic of, "Exercise," to improve the flow of energy through your body.

Keep tapping until your energy starts to improve, and you are beginning to feel and think differently about exercise. What you will notice is that once you're on the positive wing on the SUE scale, the very idea of some kind of exercise is starting to feel attractive, like something you'd actually really like to do.

And this is the master key to healthy exercise - wanting to move your body, experience your own body in movement, and finding the joy of movement again you had when you were a young child and first learned you could walk, run and skip.

We would even go so far as to advise strongly NOT to exercise until and unless you feel that you *want to move*.

- Moving the physical body against existing energy reversals always causes pain and can actually lead to injury.

This is a global principle and applies across the board - we should never do anything physical that we don't want to do against our own reversals. If the mind shouts, "No, no no!!!" and the emotions shout, "Aaargh!" the body has no chance to flow gracefully or even have its normal, natural levels of power and energy.

- We always want to empower ourselves, quite literally give us that energy we need to get up, to start feeling good, and to want to move.

If you understand the principle of empowering, energizing energy flow, you can use this to overcome resistance to exercise and find a way that is right for you to give your body, mind and spirit the exercise it needs and wants.

In conclusion, if you want to lose weight, EFT is offering you a whole new path that is actually really simple and comes back time and time again to improving the energy flow in your energy body, one way or the other.

What we all have learned and really to remember from the early weight loss EFT tappers is that keeping your energy body happy and healthy isn't a one time deal; it is something we need to do regularly and pay good attention to all the time, every day.

Over time, the baseline of empowerment in the energy system rises; that feels good but it also encourages us to go even further and to make sure that we don't just heal our energy bodies, but that we want to feed them top notch, wonderful energy foods too so they can keep shining brighter and make us happier than we've ever been before.

EFT & Will Power

There are so many people in the world today who think they have no will power, because they have tried to pitch conscious will against their own reversals and lost, time and time again.

This is a huge problem for the self concept and an erroneous assessment of the situation, based on the non-inclusion of the energy system.

When there are problems in the energy system, will power has to fail; and that is no different from someone who has a physical problem, two broken legs for example, not being able to "will themselves to walk."

Will power is a side effect of the flow of energy through the energy body. When there is good flow, we have lots of power, including will power.

When the flow is blocked, likewise, power drains away and becomes less and less in direct relationship to the energy flow getting lower and lower. This leads to loss of power in all systems - and including loss of will power.

- **If there is a lack of will power, there is a lack of <u>power</u> - full stop.**

We improve the energy flow and "power up" towards the positive side of the SUE scale, with the +10 being like a battery on full power, then we have all the will power we want.

In the past, people got stuck all the time in that ever losing battle between conscious will and the energy system, without even knowing it was their own energy system they were battling!

In all forms of addictions, for example, the addiction kicks in when power in the energy system gets dangerously low. That's when the person feels (physically) they "need something" to help them stop that slide towards disaster and so they can start to feel better again.

Now they start the battle of trying to stop themselves from taking actions which in the past have made them feel better - eating, shopping, gambling, sex, alcohol, drugs, etc. etc. etc. - with "sheer will power."

But this will power also gets lower and lower, and the whole system is already dangerously low on power overall, so the application of will power drains it even further, even faster.

This explains the observation that when will power eventually breaks down, as it will have to, the person throws themselves at the addictive behaviour or substance with even greater gusto and desperation than before.

The addiction temporarily relieves the conditions in the energy system; the person feels better, then good enough to start feeling bad about what they just did (again), and in the meantime, energy is draining away and eventually, the cycle will have to repeat itself.

- The best point of intervention from an energy standpoint is clearly *before* energy flow becomes so dangerously low in the first place.

We can imagine the day as a pipeline through time and ask where it happens that power is lost, and start tapping on that to "fix the leak."

For example, one gentleman called Ross would wake up in the morning and spend some time sitting on the bed, worrying about all the bad things that would happen in the day to come. This would leave him feeling depressed, deflated and unwilling to get up; often, he would give up on getting up and simply go back to bed, repeating this cycle numerous times before having to turn towards an addictive behaviour to get him out of bed at all, and then straight to the addiction - via an always failing battle with will power to do something else instead.

The point of first intervention in this case was clearly to get Ross to tap as soon as he woke up, to "fix that energy leakage" that was happening when he was thinking about the bad things in the day ahead.

With more energy in the system, he found that he could get up on the first attempt and start doing some of the things that needed to be done, such as getting dressed and brushing his teeth. The next energy draining point Ross found was going down the stairs and finding all the "bad letters" on the doorstep - bill payment demands, court summons and the like. Even when there were no bad letters, the walk down the stairs and the view towards the front door made him feel bad, which is the experience of energy draining away again. So he sat at the top of the stairs and tapped some more until he felt better. Ross said, "It was fascinating. All this time I never noticed, never knew that every morning I would go through all of that. I just thought I was weak, that I had no will power."

This is true in a roundabout way; he, or rather his energy system, really was weak, and as a result, did not have the energy needed to generate any form of will power either.

However, this was not a character defect as Ross had feared, nor was it a sign that Ross was a "bad person" - it was simply a sign that there were serious problems with his energy system that had never received the appropriate care and attention so he could feel better, feel "more human," as Ross put it.

In modern energy work, even having to try to assert will power over some form of existing reversal is a diagnostic that there is something wrong with the energy situation, and that action needs to be taken, and fast.

When we feel more energised, we have immediately more access to will power also - we are effectively *empowered*.

And when you're empowered, then we can really go on to say,

"Where's a will, there's a way."

EFT & The X Factor

What else could the previously mysteriously X Factor be but the energy system?

A person can have a good looking physical body, but what animates it, what makes it special, attractive, what makes it shine and glow is of course, a good looking energy system behind the scenes.

We have found that people become simply more attractive across the board when their energy system flows better.

They are easier to relate to, they feel more relaxed, friendly and loving and they can make other people feel good just by being around them.

So, how can you improve on your own X Factor?

This is really easy with EFT.

First, de-stress so you can be logical and intelligent.

Now, make a list of all your shortcomings, mental, emotional and physical. Be honest and write down everything you think is wrong with you, your mind, your body and your spirit.

Cut up the list so you've got one "what's wrong" per strip of paper, place them all into your EFT treatment bowl and treat one after the other until they've all been replaced by good and empowering feelings.

People like to try and tell us that we're wrong when we are feeling ugly but the body doesn't bear this out.

This sort of ugliness is simply a blockage in the energy system and when you take that out with EFT, and someone tells you you are beautiful, you can give them a beaming smile and say, "Absolutely! And thank you for noticing!"

There are many wonderful things about improving your X Factor with EFT.

Amongst those is that the energy system really is quite independent of the physical body; and anyone can have a beautiful, attractive, shiny energy system if they want one. It doesn't matter if they are old, deformed, scarred, broken physically - with a shiny energy system you can still get all those things that everyone dreams about, including love, respect, admiration, friendship, luck and that all important sense that one is indeed, a part of the Universe.

There is of course, more to it than that.

We don't know what an adult human being with a fully functional and evolved energy system actually feels like - it has at least been a few thousand years since such entities roamed the earth, if ever they did.

One specific detail which distinguishes the modern practice of energy work and that includes EFT is that it isn't a cult or a religion, it is strictly personal.

Each individual person gets to have their own experiences. They get to choose their own set ups, and they get to tap on their own personal problems.

This is very specific personal development of one's own energy system and where this leads, we cannot know.

A map of your own fully functional adult energy system has never been drawn; but when we get there and we do, we can be sure it will be spectacular.

Time and gravity set limits on how high we can jump, or or fast we can run.

The energy system does not have such limitations as far as we can perceive, and so it can evolve and grow stronger, more powerful and shinier for as long as we are alive.

That is a truly fascinating thought and hopefully an inspiration for you to start thinking more of your energy system, beyond all the problem solving at that, your own very special X Factor that may well have the power to solve your life's most pressing equations.

EFT & Zen States

Reaching the Zen state of mind is called by Buddhism to reach "enlightenment" or in Japanese "satori." It has been described as a higher function of mind, body and spirit in harmony, where one can think and feel at a higher level, way above the normal confusion of conscious thought; reason with brilliant clarity, know and understand with paranormal insight and act in a way that seems "superhuman" to an outsider.

Daunting though this may seem, it is actually only what happens naturally when the energy system flows at a +10 - and that is perfectly available to everyone who wants it, to anyone who has an EFT protocol handy and 15 minutes to spare.

It is true that each person's individual +10 is also not a set target, or a fixed number. The +10 grows with us, as our energy system finally starts to evolve beyond the stuck places and states that were never treated or addressed. This in turn allows us, each one of us individually, to go beyond what we could do before, and it creates new experiences we would not have had.

These new experiences - joyful and challenging alike - are then new opportunities to evolve the energy system even further; so the +10 keeps sliding along and our Healing Events become more and more amazing, as we grow.

Enlightenment is not as difficult or as rare as we have been led to believe.

Indeed, enlightenment is not a one time deal; we are designed to have many enlightenment experiences; certainly many more than people currently manage in lifetime.

At the moment, and in the context of using EFT to help our energy bodies get past the ancient blockages and into better states of energy flow, we can have our enlightenment events in the form of the Healing Events - every significant problem in the energy system offers a corresponding Healing Event that we can reach simply by tapping the SUE scale up until this wonderful thing happens and we feel as though we've just "come online" - become more enlightened.

The amazing thing is to consider that the feelings from the Healing Event, to exist at the +10 for a time, is how it is supposed to be *all the time*.

When you act from inside that energy state of +10, it doesn't matter what you do - you can shoot a bow and know the arrow will find its target, you can write poetry and know it will be mind-blowingly good; you know that if you had to run, you would run better than you have ever run before, and if you were to make love, that too would be a whole new experience.

At the moment, we are in a place where we have a Healing Event, and for time, energy is high and gives us a taste of what it's like to actually live and act with that +10 energy system providing the energy for life. Then it fades away and we're back with "normal states of being" - only these aren't really normal, they are less than what we are capable of, less than we deserve.

However, as we experience more Healing Events, and become more familiar with this territory of being at +10, we can hold that state for longer.

This is supremely important and the perfect way to conclude this book; we need to set our sights much higher than we ever did before.

Finding peace is out, experiencing true Zen states of maximum, optimum performance more often and for longer is the goal and target.

We need to learn to re-kindle our dissatisfaction and dismay at feeling anything less than that. We really do need to stop putting up with feeling low, feeling miserable, and even feeling "OK" - that's not good enough, that's not even close to what we really deserve out of life, each one of us.

Every person has their very own +10, and what that is, grows with them as the energy system develops over time and becomes more and more powerful, more and more uplifting to the mind and the body as it expands.

- **We are beings made for joy and pleasure; we are beings made for living in enlightenment.**

This has nothing to do with religion; it is just a human reality.

So we would like to leave you with the thought that it doesn't matter how old or young you are; it doesn't matter if you are rich or poor; it doesn't matter what you've been through or what you've missed out on, practical enlightenment is now within your reach.

Keep the +10 potential before you at all times and never accept second best. Never give up, and never surrender. Our amazing, undiscovered and truly wonderful energy bodies are the key to living life in splendour, and doing things better than we have ever seen them be done before.

Start with your own personal Healing Events and take it from there; and with a little experience and practice, acting in +10, achieving the mysterious Zen states where the arrow will always find its target, become not just a possibility, but an inevitable outcome of what is nothing other than practical personal development with energy in mind, body and spirit.

Addendum

A Brief History Of EFT

The principles of tapping on certain energy points to create changes were discovered by Dr Roger Callahan, a clinical psychologist of over 40 years experience, who had made it his life's work to find ways to cure people of unfounded fears, phobias, and anxieties, because he himself had suffered from these since childhood. Like any true explorer, he left no stone unturned, and finally came across some techniques, which proved to have startling repercussions.

In the much told story, he had a client named Mary who suffered from a severe phobia of water. Mary could not look at any bodies of water without experiencing extreme terror and found bathing highly traumatic, even if there was only a couple of inches of water in the tub. Dr Callahan had been working with her for 18 months, using absolutely anything and everything standard psychology and even non-standard psychology, such as hypnosis, had to offer, but she still remained afraid to death of water.

During one session in 1980 at his home in California, Dr Callahan asked Mary to tap under the eye, which is an important acupuncture/ acupressure/meridian point, and the fear just disappeared - instantaneously. It has never returned, and the treatment took place many years ago.

Dr Callahan called his discovery Thought Field Therapy (TFT for short), on the grounds that thoughts related to the energy field in the body, and that changing this energy field by tapping on the meridian points could release negative emotions rapidly and easily.

TFT treatments are based on what is called algorithms - specific sequences of tapping points to relieve specific problems.

One of Dr Callahan's students, Gary Craig, a Stanford Engineer, came up with the brilliant idea to just tap all the points for every presenting problem in 1993. There were, after all, only 13 tapping points, so whichever point or points were the correct ones, they would always be covered by default. This is an engineering technique used when a fault cannot be found – everything is replaced and the concept is known as "total redundancy." He thereby managed to create a technique that everyone can learn to use very easily and very quickly, and which does not require special diagnostic training, therapy training, or even any knowledge of the body's energy system whatever.

Gary Craig called his streamlined version "EFT - Emotional Freedom Techniques."

We take this opportunity to express my tremendous admiration for Dr Callahan who has given the world a legacy to be proud of; and to Gary Craig, who by creating the structure of EFT and making it available freely has made EFT accessible to every man and every woman.

With the onset of the Internet and from 1997 onwards, EFT began to spread rapidly around the world. This was not driven by any kind of scientific acceptance but simply by a grass root movement of individual people who tried the free EFT Classic Protocol for themselves, found that EFT worked and told others about it.

EFT triggered the formulation of the new field of "energy psychology," as most of the interested parties and originators were originally psychologists and understood EFT, TFT and the other meridian/energy based therapies available at that time as a form of new psychology tool. This caused a great increase in interest and in other forms of energy based approaches, and the foundation of two bodies dedicated to the furtherment of modern energy work, ACEP (Association for Comprehensive Energy Psychology) in the US and The AMT, (The Association for Meridian Therapies) in the UK in 1998.

Today, there are many different organisations and individuals offering various trainings and services to the modern energy work community.

In 2011, The AMT's training committee under the leadership of Silvia Hartmann adopted the new, energy orientated EFT Heart & Soul Protocol to replace the original Classic EFT Protocol as the standard EFT teaching protocol to reflect the learnings and experiences with EFT in the field over the preceding 15 years.

Modern energy work, as demonstrated by EFT, is no longer considered to be an adjunct of psychology; it is deemed to be a field in its own right, the Third Field in the mind/body/spirit triad.

The Third Field addresses neither mental health, nor physical health, but instead the important topic of energy body health and well-being, which is foundational and without which a truly holistic treatment of many, if not all, human problems simply cannot exist.

We encourage all who love EFT and have personally satisfied themselves through their own experiences of the effectiveness of EFT in the treatment of energy body related problems to become an active part in this new and emerging field, to continue their education, their personal exploration and to take part in conferences and online communities.

The Association For Meridian & Energy Therapies is a Learned Society which any person who is interested in modern energy work can join and which offers information, professional trainings and conferences in modern energy work and including EFT Emotional Freedom Techniques.

To become a member of The AMT, for up to date information, trainings and practitioners of EFT, please visit:

www.TheAMT.com

Join TheAMT at Associate Member or Professional Level:
http://TheAMT.com/join.htm

Find an EFT Master Practitioner:
http://TheAMT.com/eft_master_practitioners/

Find a live EFT/Energy Training Event:
http://TheAMT.com/events/

Study EFT by Distance Learning:
http://TheAMT.com/courses/

The Annual International EFT/Energy Conference:
http://TheAMT.com/conference/

Evolving The EFT Protocol

From Classic EFT To EFT Heart & Soul

When the original or Classic EFT Protocol was devised, it was very unclear how EFT really worked, and the simplicity of working with the energy body wasn't fully understood. There was talk of Thought Fields, algorithms and a general confusion as to what was happening or why; and the original Classic EFT Protocol reflected a mixture of ideas, patterns and techniques in use at the time in the psychology and kinesiology communities.

The original Classic EFT Protocol started with a set up which was cushioned inside the opening statement of, "Even though ... I deeply and profoundly love and accept myself."

This cushion around the actual problem was put there to avoid the client abreacting or "falling into" the problem too deeply; but it was learned in the practice of doing EFT with many clients that the cushion caused confusion, often a negative response from people who said, "I just have a fear of spiders, I'm not interested in loving and accepting myself!"

It was further realised that the cushion also confused the "tuning in" process of finding the right space/time address in the very complex energy system, which has to be as specific and precise as possible in order to get the best results. With the addition of the centring and stabilising Heart Healing Posture, the fear of abreaction was alleviated and so in the modern Heart & Soul Protocol, we can simply state the problem, or preface all EFT treatments with treatment rounds for "Stress," to make EFT treatments elegant, stress free and easy.

In the Heart & Soul Protocol, apart from the extremely important Heart Healing Posture, three further points were added.

These are:

- The Top Of The Head or Crown point/s, which are a natural exit/entrance place for many of the most important energy flows in the energy body;

- the Third Eye point which is the connector to the psychic circuitry or strange flows;

- and the Ring Finger, simply to alleviate the endless questions as to "why don't we tap on the ring finger?" and to make the EFT round more logical and more intuitive.

The treatment points that were left out were

- the Sore Spot which represented a significant disruption in the EFT treatment process, particularly with beginners,

- the Gamut Point, which was used in the original protocol during the 9 Gamut Treatment

- the Under Arm Point was dropped to improve ease of the treatment flow.

The entire 9 Gamut Treatment was removed, which involved tapping on the Gamut point whilst rolling the eyes around (at the time the original protocol was devised, EMDR (Eye Movement Desensitization and Reprocessing) was popular in the psychologist's community) and singing a song, for example, "Happy Birthday."

This had very little to do with simple, direct modern energy work and used to represent a significant problem in the presentation of EFT to the general public, knowledgeable energists and the scientifically minded alike.

The Classic EFT protocol was called an "EFT Sandwich" because it involved one round of EFT, then the 9 Gamut treatment, then another round of EFT.

By using the simplified Heart & Soul EFT Protocol, we have in essence twice the time and more to discuss significant and specific set ups. We can do two rounds with evolving set ups in the same time frame; plus the deletion of the 9 Gamut treatment has significantly improved the uptake and reaction to the protocol, especially in new people.

The biggest difference overall in the evolution of the EFT protocol is to recognise and be clear about that *this is an energy treatment*, designed to affect the energy body. This in conjunction with the centring effects of the new Heart & Soul EFT protocol, its ease of use and the design which is focused on improving energy flow all the way has led to significant advances in the speed, effectiveness and uptake of the practice of EFT as a modern energy modality.

For more information on the EFT Heart & Soul Protocol, to view a Classic EFT protocol and learn more about the changes to the EFT protocols, as well as the latest updates on Energy EFT, please visit

www.1-EFT.com

From SUD To SUE - Bringing Joy To EFT

When EFT was first formulated by Gary Craig in the 1990s, a measurement scale, inherited from medicine via psychology called the SUD scale was used to help guide and test EFT sessions.

The SUD scale, Subjective Units of Discomfort, also sometimes called Subjective Units of Distress or Disturbance, was originally designed to measure physical pain as the patient felt it inside. Logically, the scale went from -10 which was the highest form of pain to Zero, where no pain was felt any longer.

This was and is a good scale to measure how much physical pain a person is in; however, working with energy and emotions, it was learned that this scale was not only not enough to describe emotional experiences, but *its very usage was placing unnecessary limitations and even blocks to real evolution into the treatment flow of modern energy work.*

People do not just experience negative emotions; and indeed, it is the experience of positive emotions, high positive emotions at that, which are the goal, benchmark and test for energy body based interventions.

The SUE Scale (Subject Units of Experience, Hartmann 2009) was therefore necessary: measuring from -10, via 0 (the Zero Point of Nothing) to +10, the high energized end states that come about when a Healing Event in the energy system has taken place.

The difference between the SUD scale and the SUE scale demonstrates the profound difference that exists between old and modern approaches to energy work in a nutshell.

By bringing in the positive wing of the SUE scale, it was now possible not just to explain the previously mysterious and unpredictable "One Minute Wonder" EFT effects, but to structurally plot a path for every treatment session, no matter what the topic or problem might be, to achieve a Healing Event by continuously improving the energy flow towards +10, even if it takes more than one session.

This raises the bar for EFT treatments; but more, it also alleviates many of the problems that dodged EFT treatments in the past, when treatments stopped too soon and left people in an "emotional no-man's land" and unwilling/incapable of understanding what had happened to them.

Leaving the EFT treatments unfinished, before a Healing Event had taken place, also led to the problem recurring, as well as amnesia and Apex Effect (a person feeling better but having no connection with the EFT treatment that caused the improvement). There were further follow on problems, such as people being unwilling to "tap important emotions away" for fear of losing something; people rightfully feeling that "feeling nothing" is not a good place to be; and people being less than delighted with their EFT treatments at the end and finding little motivation to do more EFT, or seek further treatments.

There are many problems avoided by understanding the nature of energy work as demonstrated by the SUE scale with that all important wing of positive emotions that get more powerful, the better the energy flow becomes.

As good as this is, the most important message of the SUE scale is that we don't seek nothing, but joy instead.

- **The SUE scale brings joy into modern energy work, not just symptom cessation.**

This is a true paradigm shift which does not just affect the spirit, but also the mind and the body too through the intimate connections that exist in the human totality.

Where before the idea and hope was to go through life and experience as little pain as possible, we are now in a position to raise our expectations and aim directly for having as much good emotions as possible - feeling joy, love, hope, excitement, pleasure in our own bodies.

This is what energizes our lives, literally; this is what we need to inspire us, empower us, and gives us the strength to do what we need to do, every day.

The practice of EFT demonstrates that without a shadow of a doubt, every one of us can feel *better* - feel more powerful positive emotions, no matter who we are, or where we came from.

This is a wonderful gift, encompassed in the SUE scale in a nutshell.

The Professional EFT Practitioner

Working with EFT as a modern energy modality is a truly extraordinary opportunity to help people in a way they have never been helped before.

Psychology and medicine have struggled to give the support and solution every day people need to overcome the many challenges in our modern world, and *the human energy body has never received the positive attention it deserves and needs to function properly*.

There are all manner of problems where EFT could alleviate the symptoms and make life easier for the people who suffer from them; but there are also many, many problems that can't be solved at all until and unless we take the energy body into consideration.

Whether this is a person dying of a broken heart; a teenager being driven into suicide by sheer stress; a soldier crippled with the ravages of PTSD or a man beating his wife yet again because he doesn't know what to do to be able to stop or a mathematician staring at the same equation for decades, unable to know how to solve this, there are myriads of instances where EFT can give us evolution where nothing else could.

As modern energy work, EFT is neither medicine or psychology, and an EFT practitioner relates to their clients in a very different way than a doctor or a therapist would.

Being connected, being in rapport and experiencing how energy changes as it starts to flow is of the essence in doing EFT with other people. Instead of an all powerful healer up on high, and a helpless client down below, when people do EFT together, they form what we call the EFTeam - an alliance of two equal, honest human beings who both hold the heartfelt intention to improve energy flow and help each other feel better.

Being an EFT practitioner and experiencing other people's relief, then joy and delight first hand in full rapport, makes helping other people with EFT into a wonderful experience that lifts the practitioner as much as it does the client. Modern energy work really is quite unlike healing and therapy of old; and EFT is a gift that keeps on giving, not just for the client, but for the practitioner, every time a Healing Event is achieved.

We therefore encourage existing therapists and holistic healers to take up the practice of EFT as an adjunct to their existing practices; but also to encourage those who long wanted to help others to come forward and consider training to become a professional EFT practitioner.

The AMT offers a variety of live trainings as well as an official distance learning course which will eventually enable the student to start practising EFT professionally in their chosen field of endeavour.

As time goes by, more and more people are becoming aware of modern energy work, of which EFT is often the first ambassador.

To discover more about becoming a professional EFT practitioner, please visit

www.TheAMT.com

EFT In The Third Field

When EFT first started out, it was thought to be a helpful tool for psychology or a psychology method.

Over the last 15 years, we have discovered that EFT is in fact, modern energy work and therefore belongs in the Third Field of the mind/body/spirit triad.

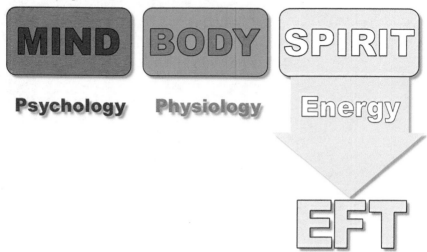

Although everybody talks about the mind/body/*spirit* triad, and there are few left on Earth today who would actively deny the existence of there being more to life than current science may be able to measure, it is still deemed to be unscientific to even try to research and explore the Third Field.

This clearly has to change; if the practice of EFT by so many people has taught us anything, it has taught us that the human race cannot go on any longer trying to ignore the human experience of emotion and the reality of the human energy body.

The application of EFT and other highly modern and original energy techniques, such as EmoTrance, has proven beyond the shadow of a doubt that if we want to solve problems, we need to do so with a clear mind; if we want to solve conflicts, we need to be doing so with a clarity of emotional states; and if we want to tackle the myriad of problems we have inherited from our ancestors, we need to approach the human condition in a new and different way.

In short, we cannot get by without the energy system and dealing with it, trying to understand it, and working directly with energy through modern modalities such as EFT.

Likewise, we are now at a stage where nothing can be gained by trying to pretend that EFT is some kind of psychology, a trick of the mind, a behavioural disruption pattern, or hypnosis.

Many people are afraid that if they were to come out of the energy closet and state that they are in fact energists when working with EFT, they would be called charlatans, snake oil salesmen and unscientific.

It is true that this can happen at this time; however, there are now too many people around who have experienced the reality of the human energy system, the reality of their own emotions and how those affect their thoughts, behaviour and performance.

The energy cat is out of the bag, we might say.

This is a good thing, and especially a good thing for those who wish to share the joy of EFT, the simplicity of it, and the wonderful benefits the application of EFT brings to people's lives.

EFT, viewed as some kind of slightly bizarre and esoteric method from the murkier, dubious edges of psychology, was already a great improvement on what there was before.

- **EFT, viewed clearly as a foundational technique for the Third Field of modern energy work, is a paradigm shift.**

When we apply EFT with energy in mind, we gain access to the positive side of the SUE Scale - that place of empowerment, when the "batteries are full," when a person comes to life, and finally becomes aware of the true extent of their own powers, resources, talents and abilities in mind, body and spirit.

When we apply EFT with energy in mind, we can approach all manner of human problems that seemed so impossible to solve with confidence, with curiosity and most of all, with evolution in mind.

You can tap EFT just as a ritual, without thought, without a care, and benefits will ensue.

But if you tap EFT with a full knowledge that it is your own healing hands working on your energy body to release blockages and sooth disturbances and injuries, the benefits likewise are a paradigm shift further to what was there before.

This is perfectly true for self help; and even more so when we become EFT practitioners and help others.

Working with energy *and knowing that you do* creates a completely different dynamic between the practitioner and the client than would be found in medicine or in psychology, the other two fields already in existence to serve the citizen and help them lead happier, healthier lives.

The Third Field has its own ways of working. It has its own code of conduct between client and practitioner; it has its own methods, such as EFT and EmoTrance. It has its own instruments, such as the SUE Scale, and all of these derive directly from the essential differences of working with the energy system.

We encourage all practitioners of modern energy work, be they practising in self help or in professional practice, to be proud of what they do; to understand that the Third Field is highly important, absolutely essential for the future development of the human race and to go forward with their own explorations, their own personal experiences without fear.

Whether energy bodies really exist, or whether energy is just a metaphor that works spectacularly well with human beings, either way, the Third Field is here, and if you do EFT, you have become a part of it.

By all means, treat yourself for reversals and blockages relating to the idea of working with energy, and you being "an energist."

Modern energy work is logical, straightforward and so immensely beneficial that we really do need to share it, to stand up for it and essentially to be proud and delighted to be a part of what has to be a true grass roots revolution way beyond the invention of the printing press.

- **Getting to grips with our own emotions is what the human race needs.**

Finally understanding and mastering our emotions is exactly what we need to progress beyond what there is today, and what there has been for the last 100,000 years of human history.

Anyone who tackles that subject, individually or professionally, is doing something right, something to be very proud of, something to be very excited about.

The more of us come out of that energy closet and stand up and say, "Yes, I'm an energist!" the sooner many more tears will remain uncried, many more battles will remain unfought, and more intelligence, joy, logic and love will enter the world of human beings at large.

There isn't a single area of human endeavour that can't be improved upon now with the application of modern energy work; there isn't a single problem that can't at least be evolved forward from the places people have got stuck in.

Modern energy work is really that important; EFT as its first ambassador is that important; and we are here, at the beginning of the Third Field, each one of us an important participant, each one of us who experiences more love and joy in their life an uplifting to us all.

In that spirit, I would personally like to wish you many more wonderful freeing and truly delightful energy experiences than you ever hoped for and remain with my best wishes,

Silvia Hartmann

January 1st, 2012

About The Author

Silvia Hartmann was born in Germany in 1959 and emigrated to the United Kingdom in 1978. She became fascinated with animal behaviour and spent 15 years training and practising as an animal behaviour specialist. During a study on Attention Seeking Behaviour Disorders In Social Mammals, Silvia Hartmann became aware of the existence of energy exchanges which are crucial to the health and well being of social mammals. Her foundational thesis on the subject, The Harmony Program, was published in 1993.

The structure of energetic relationships and the importance of energy exchanges to general health and well being of social mammals clearly included human beings as well. From 1993 onwards, Silvia Hartmann turned her attention to discovering more about how energy works in the human context, and importantly, how language, energy and metaphor interact in the human consciousness. This produced "Project Sanctuary," a working method designed to improve energy flow between the conscious mind and the energy mind (previously known as the un- or subconscious mind), and the original Energetic Relationships papers. In 1998, Silvia Hartmann came across Gary Craig's EFT and spent four years intensively researching the cause and effect of using this energy based intervention. In 2002, she published her findings and proposed a new method of working with energy, EmoTrance (Emotional Transformation). EmoTrance contains the basic theory of modern energy work and is both a research tool in its own right as well as a foundational method to work with energy occurrences beyond resolving existing blockages in the energy body.

For the next ten years, EmoTrance was tested in practice and helped to illuminate many significant structural principles of modern energy work. These included the discovery of the Guiding Stars (2002), highly charged positive events which cause addictions; the Energized End States which are the foundation of modern energy work and the SUE scale, and eventually, Events Psychology (2009), which explains the cause and effect of energy body events and belief formation in human beings.

In 2011, Silvia Hartmann was tasked to create a new EFT training for the Association of Meridian & Energy Therapies The AMT. After consulting with the AMT trainers, it was decided to build into the next generation of EFT the many gains and advances from EmoTrance and Events Psychology, and to re-design the EFT protocol with energy in mind.

Silvia Hartmann is a member of the United Kingdom Society of Authors and trainings director for The Association For Meridian & Energies Therapies.

For more information about her work, please visit

www.SilviaHartmann.com

Further Reading

Events Psychology

How To Understand Yourself & Other People

DragonRising 2009 - ISBN 978-1873483657

EmoTrance

Emotions, Energy, Information & Love

DragonRising 2011 - ISBN 978-1873483510

The Genius Symbols

Learn To Communicate With Your Energy Mind

DragonRising 2011 - ISBN 978-1873483695

Available from all good book stores, online and off
and directly from
www.DragonRising.com

Alphabetical Index